Understand the English,
A personal A-Z

Understanding the English,
A personal A-Z

ALAN MACFARLANE

2019

First published in Great Britain
by Cam Rivers Publishing Ltd
2019

Devised by Zilan Wang
Written by Alan Macfarlane
Typesetting and layout design by Jaimie Norman
Marketing Manager James O'Sullivan

Written text © Alan Macfarlane 2019
© Cam Rivers Publishing 2019

All rights reserved.

This publication has been generously supported by the Kaifeng Foundation.

The moral rights of Alan Macfarlane have been asserted in accordance with the Copyright, Designs and Patents Act, 1988. No part of this publication may be reproduced, stored in or introduced into a retrieval system, or transmitted, in any form or by any means (electronic, mechanical, photocopying, recording or otherwise), without prior written permission of the copyright owner. This book is sold subject to the condition that it shall not, by way of trade or otherwise, be lent, re-sold, hired out, or otherwise circulated without the publisher's prior consent in any form of binding or cover other than that in which it is published and without a similar condition including this condition being imposed on the subsequent purchaser.

Printed and Bound in Great Britain.

ISBN 978-1-093734-72-0

www.cambridgerivers.com
press@cambridgerivers.com

Contents

Preface   1
Why should we bother to understand the English?   4
Why is England so difficult to understand?   7

Some features: A-Z   12

Amateurs   13
Antiquities   14
Aplomb   15

Barter   17
Beef   18
Beer   19
Brexit   20
Bribery   21
Bureaucracy   22

Ceremonial   24
Christmas   25
Cleanliness   26
Cliques   26
Clubs   31
Coal   28
Common sense   29
Communities   30
Crime   31

Decency   33

Eating   34
Education   35
Equality   36
Ethics   37
Etiquette   38
Evil   39

Fair Play   41
Fishing and hunting   42
Folk culture   42
Footpaths and parks   43
Foreigners   44
Fourth estate   45

Gentlemen	47
Gifts	48
Green	49
Greetings and gestures	50
Happiness	51
History	52
Hobbies	53
Holidays	54
Honour and shame	55
Horses	55
Inconvenience	57
Individualism	58
Inns, houses and churches	59
Justice and fairness	61
Kindness	62
Language	64
Lavatories	65
Liberty	66
London	67
Manners	68
Masks	69
Men	70
Muddle	70
Night fears	72
Oak trees	73
Patronage	75
Personal records	76
Pets	76
Philistine	77
Positivism and empiricism	78
Privacy	79
Queuing	81
Revolution	82
Restlessness	83
Rites of passage	84
Royal family	84
Seas	86
Secrets and lies	86

Security	87
Service	88
Sex	90
Shooting and weapons	90
Spartan	91
Summer	92
Sweet and bitter	93
Taboo	94
Taxation	95
Tea and sugar	96
Time	97
Trust	98
Truth	99
Understatement and modesty	101
United Kingdom	102
Universities	102
Urbanism	103
Utopia	104
Violence	106
Weather	108
Women	108
Xanadu and gardens	111
Yes and no	113
Young and old	114
Zen	115
Some cultural rules by which I live	116
Some further reading on the English A-Z	120
My books on the English	121
Acknowledgements	122
Notes to text	123

Preface

I think of myself as both an insider and an outsider as far as the English are concerned. I am an *insider* because nearly three-eighths of my genetic heritage is English, because I have lived mainly in England since the age of five (seventy-two years) and because I was educated to be English through my family, schools and universities.

I am an *outsider* because five-eighths of my heritage is Scots, with a touch of Welsh, because I was born and brought up for five years in India, and because I have spent much of my life as an anthropologist working in Nepal (during fifty years), in Japan (during almost thirty years) and in China (during twenty-three years) and in teaching about all the civilizations around the world.

I realize late in my life that I have spent the last seventy years, since I came back from India as a small child in 1947, trying to understand my own, English, civilization. I have devoted much of my professional life as a historian and anthropologist to thinking about who this island people really are. I have published more than a dozen books around the theme of Englishness, as listed in the bibliography at the end. I have lectured around the world, and constantly talked to my friends and students about the subject.

Now is the time to gather these fragmented understandings together in the hope that they will be useful to others, both to the English themselves and to the many who visit England or view it from the outside. To all of them, it may be helpful to know how this old and complex civilization, which has given—by force in some cases—the world many of its central features – industrialization, capitalism, democracy, language, games and much more – looks to an insider/outsider.

Because there are so many contradictions and enigmas (as explained a little more under the first entry 'Absurdity'), I have decided that I will try an approach in which I treat the English like a jigsaw puzzle, stained-glass window or mosaic floor. I take a number of features which have puzzled, amused or interested me in other ways, and explain very briefly the enigma and, where necessary, the causes behind it. Of course, there are many others which my friends have pointed out to me and would be fun to look at. Yet books tend to grow and grow, so I have stopped here.

There are dozens of books about the English, yet almost all of them describe the chosen features – queuing, cricket, pubs, pets or whatever – without explaining what <u>causes</u> them. If we don't understand <u>why</u> the English queue, trust each other on the whole, love their pets, it is less easy to appreciate the inter-connections in the patterns of their culture, or to deal with the situations we meet.

Obviously, everyone in England is different. The way I look at this as a seventy-six-year old, white, male, middle-class, privileged, university-educated, academic who has spent much of his recent years travelling the world, will be different from that of everyone else. Yet I hope that the fact that I look at the English both from the inside and outside, will give the interpretation some universality.

I am myself more than half Scottish in my ancestry, with some Welsh also thrown in. For these reasons, I am particularly aware of the problem of whether I am writing of the English or the British. I have decided to call the subject 'the English' because there are special features of that part of the United Kingdom. Yet I am obviously also aware that perhaps three quarters of what I write could also be held to be true of the rest of Britain.

I am also aware that the English have been made by many other peoples, including the Scots, Welsh and Irish. Yet in this time of heightened sensibility about national identities, with votes to dismember larger unities, it seems the least of evils to call the book the English, rather than the British.

If you look up 'The English people' on *Wikipedia* you will find that they 'are a nation and an ethnic group native to England who speak the English language'. Currently they number about eighty to a hundred million around the world, with about thirty-seven million in the U.K. and the rest mainly in the United States, Australia and Canada.

From this it can be seen that there are many other groups of importance in the U.K. and even in England. This book is about one small group in the world, and one of many groups in the U.K. It is therefore not a picture of England today, but of a set of people who think of themselves as 'English', although, of course, almost all of them have ancestry from other parts of the world.

It is also a picture of a rapidly changing world and parts of it reflect features which are rapidly disappearing. The England I encountered when I landed as a small boy from India in 1947 is hugely different in almost every aspect from the England today. I have written, as anthropologists often do, about a vanishing world, writing in the present tense though some features are already shifting. It is as much a piece of rescue or salvage anthropology as it is a current guide to the English wherever they live.

Finally, I would like to thank Fabienne Bonnet, sometime Chaplain of Homerton College, Cambridge and Lectrice at King's College, Cambridge. She checked the text and made a number of comments, written from the point of view of a native French observer who has spent forty-five years living in the U.K.

Why should we bother to understand the English?

A reader may wonder, beyond the prompting of mere curiosity, or a desire or need to get along in England or with English people, why the English should merit attention nowadays. It is true that Britain once ruled the largest empire in history, but those days are well over and England and the U.K. are now a somewhat peripheral, small, peoples on the edge of a Continent. Even if their reputation and membership of various world bodies like the Security Council of the U.N. makes them disproportionately big players, the reasons for wanting to understand them is deeper than this.

Basically, anyone in the world, and particularly of course in parts of the former British Empire, including the United States, needs to understand England to understand the modern world in which we live. This is because over the last half millenium many of the foundations of modernity were laid by people from this little island. These ideas were often derived from outside England, but were reshaped and then propagated around the world through the British Empire. This is succinctly put by Claudio Veliz, and described in his book. 'It is possible to affirm that regardless of country of origin or place of residence, ourselves and our contemporaries were all born and live today in a world made in England...'[1]

The system of parliamentary, representative, democracy comes from England and is the ideal for many people around the world. The dominant political idea for our world comes from England. Even its major alternative, communism, was devised in England and specifically in the Reading Room of the British Library by Karl Marx.

The central part of the economic system of the world, market capitalism, was developed over the centuries in Britain. The ideas of private property, banking, multi-purpose money, bills and bonds and shares, the freedom to exchange, the separation out of the economy from politics religion and the family, were British ideas. The first three great classical economists, Adam Smith, Thomas Malthus and David Ricardo all worked in Britain.

The international language of the world is English and even with the rise of Chinese Mandarin, is likely to remain so. This has helped to propagate the influence of English ideas and also English literature. Many people around the world study the poetry, novels and essays, as well as the extraordinary children's stories written by English (and Scottish and Irish) writers.

The modern world is now based on another English/British invention, the industrial revolution, that is the replacing of human and other natural energy by fossil fuels with machines and then later technology. This revolution was a continuation of a long tradition in England of using non-human energy from wind, water, coal and animals and combining them with systematic and scientific farming through an agricultural revolution. More recently, the current technological revolution in computing and artificial intelligence was invented by English men and women from Charles Babbage and Ada Lovelace through to Alan Turing, Tim Berners-Lee and Sophie Wilson.

This takes us to other parts of science and technology, where the great figures of English thought, Francis Bacon, Isaac Newton, Caroline Herschel, Charles Darwin, through to Rosalind Franklin, Thomas Crick and James Watson, have contributed hugely to our present world.

In terms of organizational structures, the English have developed many of the philanthropic and social institutions which have spread everywhere, the Boy Scouts and Girl Guides, the Samaritans, Oxfam and many others. The 'League of Nations', which led into the United Nations, was also devised in England.

One of England's greatest exports has been in the field of leisure. Not only the important team games like football, cricket and rugby, but many other sports and past-time such as rock-climbing, organized horse racing, swimming, had their rules and customs formalized in England.

Part of the reason for this was the widespread growth of associations or clubs, small groups of like-minded individuals who pooled their wealth and efforts in the pursuit of a goal. The clubs, and the pubs or public houses which are so distinctively English, along with a unique system of self-rule through devolved local government, provided the bedrock of freedom. They created a strong protection for individual citizens, what we call 'civil society', another English invention.

Another form of these clubs and trusts shaped the educational system of England. The English boarding school for young people is the oldest English institution, going back 1,400 years. Later it would flourish in the famous schools and universities of Britain which still attract many students and many imitators and has shaped education in the United States and elsewhere.

The schools and universities took children out of their families and placed them in a wider society and economy. They were free to choose their own partners for life and hence this is linked to another world influencing system, the nuclear family, with children leaving home to be independent, and the basing of marriage upon romantic love.

None of the above is written to diminish the contribution of other civilizations. Indeed, it is equally easy to argue that the English are really a mixture of Arabic, Indian, Chinese or Dutch influences, as much as the other way around. Nevertheless, it is true that for a crucial few centuries, the path to our modern world temporarily mainly passed through this little island. So, if we wish to understand ourselves anywhere in the world, as well as to enjoy contacts in the U.K., it is worth spending a little time and effort trying to understand the English.

Why are the English so difficult to understand?

When the great political theorist Alexis de Tocqueville studied and wrote about America, France and England, he found it very easy to understand America – recent and laid out symmetrically on the basis of some simple principles. France was more complex, but he could grasp it. Yet he wrote of England that, despite many visits and being married to an English wife, it was beyond his understanding.

> 'It would take a very fatuous philosopher to imagine that he could understand England in six months. A year has ever seemed to me too short a time for a proper appreciation of the United States, and it is infinitely easier to form clear ideas and precise conceptions about America than about Great Britain.'[2]

Why, then is it so difficult? Surely England is small, with a uniform language, laws, economic and political system and even weather?

There are several reasons for the difficulty, some of them deriving from the fact that England is a middle-sized island. This island influence is confirmed by the fact that a certain amount of what I write here can also apply to Japan, another extraordinarily difficult place to understand.

Both islands were defended by their seas and hence have seldom, if ever, been conquered. The last conquest of Britain was in 1066 by the Normans and the Normans became absorbed into the Anglo-Saxon population and social patterns. When combined with the absence of serious, rule-changing, revolutions in either island, we see before us in both England and Japan a very old and convoluted tree that has grown and become ever more dense, knotted and inter-twined over more than a thousand years. Old ways are modified, partly covered over, but not systematically wiped away. Compromises are constantly being made and there is evolution rather than revolution, a child growing into an adult yet preserving much of the child.

The result is that there are endless anomalies, inconsistencies, redundancies, little bits and pieces left-over and creating roughness. These are most visible in public rituals and ceremonies – a Coronation, Royal Wedding, Opening of Parliament or Degree Ceremony. These enigmas infuse all of life and an outsider can constantly be tripped up or confused by a seemingly pointless, half-obscured, barrier or custom.

The situation is exacerbated by the fact that England is a customary, oral, culture. English law is based on custom and precedent, and much of English culture is unspoken, never articulated or formalized. From the absence of a written constitution, to the importance of precedent, the English know how to ride the bicycle of their culture through practice, through long socialization within it, but not through any explicit code.

Hence, they know, as with their baffling grammar and language, when something seems right or wrong, but they often cannot explain why. It is therefore almost impossible to write a guide to Englishness since it is so deep, but obscured and covered over. It is similar to what the French call *habitus*, something which generates much thought and behaviour but which cannot be approached or addressed directly.

The situation is further compounded by another factor. The essence of Englishness, and of the modernity which it has given the world, is based on tensions and contradictions that have never been resolved. This is what makes England free, creative, energetic and attractive, yet it is also very difficult to grasp.

This presence of in-built contradictions and anomalies is something which struck many observers. Emerson wrote of 'The English composite character betrays a mixed origin. Everything English is a fusion of distant and antagonistic elements.' (Emerson, Traits, 42), adding later Anomalies of England. '...but England subsists by antagonisms and contradictions... from first to last, it is a museum of anomalies.' (Emerson, Traits, 75). Orwell put it in another way: "the Englishman is a symbol of the strange mixture of reality and illusion, democracy and privilege, humbug and decency, the subtle network of compromises, by which the nation keeps itself in its familiar shape". [3]

The result, as the philosopher and Scotsman David Hume wisely observed, is that there really is no such thing as English national identity, unless the absence of such uniformity can be seen as the quintessential identity.

> 'We may often remark on wonderful mixture of manners and characters in the same nation... the English government is a mixture of monarchy,

aristocracy, and democracy. The people in authority are composed of gentry and merchants. All sects of religion are to be found among them. And the great liberty and independency, which every man enjoys, allows him to display the manners peculiar to him. Hence the English, of any people in the universe, have the least of a national character; unless this very singularity may appear to pass for such.'[4]

One way of addressing the difficulty of dealing with fundamental contradictions is to consider the four great human drives, the desire for *power* (politics), *wealth* (economics), *human warmth* (society) and *meaning* (religion and ideology). In most societies these overlap, usually in the family, sometimes in an attempted fusion such as communism. Thus, in great continents like China or India, there was no embedded choice or conflict between family, religion, work and politics.

In England and other parts of the world, in becoming modern, the individual rather than the family becomes the basis of the civilization and the individual is the one who has to find a personal balance between the push and pull of these different forces. There is always a choice and always a trade-off and sacrifice. The religious devotee sacrifices wealth and family, the businessman may sacrifice family and morality. The effect can be loneliness, constant striving, ambivalence and uncertainty, but also release and freedom.

Life for many becomes a constant struggle to obtain as much as possible on each, or at least several of these fronts, but there is unlikely to be final contentment. This constant and highly personal struggle also means constant changes of direction, hence the reputation of the English as hypocritical and changeable and their nickname 'perfidious Albion'. This also links with the idea of structured competition, albeit within a set of rules, because playing a complex game—whether in politics, the market, law, the pursuit of truth or the pursuit of virtue—is central to English culture.

The effect of this is that if one examines any part of the English system, as is also the case with Japan, it is possible to argue for very opposed interpretations. The English are very peaceful, calm, civilized, loving gardens, poetry, friendship and generally law-abiding. Yet they are also highly warlike abroad and often very aggressive.

The English emphasize equality, not only of the rich and poor, women and men, children and adults, black and white. Yet they also have the strongest class system in the world and were great slave traders.

The English have been deeply interested in religion and their poetry, philosophy, novels, art and even architecture is still deeply shaped by Christianity. Yet they cannot agree on anything about God, a country of a thousand sects (religious groups), but only one sauce (cooking style) as opposed to France with one sect, but a thousand sauces. 'The only point on which there is general agreement is that nearly every Englishman holds a different belief; all of them believe in some particular point peculiar to themselves.'[5]

Religion, while all pervasive, is a private matter, not something you should talk about too much in polite societies, though much of the missionizing around the world was undertaken under British influence.

Or again, the British were early an industrial and urban civilization, polluting and dirty, controlling the natural world to an unprecedented degree. Alongside this they are famed for their love of nature, gardens, animals and wildness. The paradoxes are endless and difficult for an outsider to understand.

In this very short introduction I can only suggest a few clues. As a child coming back from India to boarding schools in England I had to learn how to be properly English – not just the myths and rituals of this ancestral if distant tribe, but the games, social codes and cultural rules that governed and shaped human interaction. I absorbed them in the same way as I learnt to swim or ride a bicycle, through practice.

Here I will try to unlearn, or at least bring back to the surface what I learnt. It is a tricky task, but made a little easier by the fact that I became an anthropologist. In my many visits to Nepal, Japan and China, the invisible air or water that had surrounded me from my socialization in the system became a little visible through placing what I thought and did against the backdrop of other cultures. So perhaps something of what I write will help others to understand a little of the riddle, mystery and enigma of the English.

One final difficulty is worth making explicit. This is to know who the English are. Who is this book about?

England has for centuries been absorbing people from other cultures, invasions both warlike and peaceful. The result is that 'the

English' were always a mongrel race. Then for two centuries, from the middle of the eighteenth to middle of the twentieth, Britain ruled the greatest Empire on earth and was flooded with ideas, artefacts and, to a lesser extent, people from all corners of the earth. It was a cosmopolitan, world, civilization.

Ironically, the loss of its Empire after the Second World War has not diminished but increased the inflow of ideas, objects and people and the England of today is very different indeed to the England forty years ago. As of March 2019, of the total of fifty-six million in England and Wales, white people number roughly forty-eight and a quarter million (86%), but of these at least a million are from Europe. Then there are four and roughly a quarter million from Asia, one million 864,000 black and one million and 224,000 of mixed race.

While white 'English' are still the large majority, there are numerous other sizeable communities. Even in my own fairly remote fenland village, over the last three years and I have noticed that people from all over the world are coming to live here. Immigrants from other cultures have changed 'the English' themselves in basic ways, in food, clothing, music, language and religion, among much else.

It is therefore impossible, and indeed a waste of time, to try to isolate what is genuinely, deeply, 'English' and what is 'foreign'. The best we can do is to think of Britain, and England within it, as a complex painting or jigsaw. It is composed of an infinite set of coloured variations and shapes, yet it mostly works in the task of unifying them into a picture.

All this is important in reading this book. Each person will have a different experience of 'English people'. My ideas reflect my limited experience – based on my gender, class, education, job, the timing of my life since 1941. I have tried to broaden this very particular experience by reading and studying history and anthropology and by looking at the English from outside, from Nepal, Japan and China.

Others will naturally see another 'English people' and may find parts of what I write to be over-idealistic, over-simple, biased, and even old-fashioned. No matter, for all we can do is to write as we see it and leave others to decide how far this helps in the understanding and managing of their daily lives.

A-Z

Amateurs

Most civilizations and societies ensure that their important positions are held by highly trained professionals, carefully prepared for the job. They also tend to believe that those making a great effort in some activity should be directly rewarded, preferably with money or other goods. The culture of the amateur in England goes against both of these almost universal tendencies.

The English, of course, have professional training. Yet much of their education is concerned with producing people who can move easily from one type of skilled activity to another. An extreme example is their political system in which a person can one moment be in charge of a huge department concerned with health or education, the next day move to transport or law. It is widely believed that almost anybody can do anything, that the application of personality and common sense will make it possible to master new skills in a few days, that you will quickly 'learn on the job'.

Likewise, there is the cult of the amateur, particularly in sports and games. For long periods in the past, though in the last few decades this has been changing rapidly, people played for the social and physical rewards and not for money. In much of the legal system (magistrates), administration (local government) and other parts of the system, the work is done by unpaid amateurs, not specially trained and yet expected to be effective.

Understanding this amateur streak is important when considering how to interact with the English. They admire the versatile, the flexible, the agile…in other words the person who bothers when there is no monetary reward. Narrow, over-professional, pedantic, money-seeking is to be avoided.

Antiquities

Antiquities refer to old things, whether buildings, small pieces of furniture or jewellery. One of the things that strikes visitors to England is their love of these old things. They write books called *On Living in an Old Country* (Patrick Wright, 1985) and are proud to do so. This antiquity is not only to be seen in their old churches, houses, woods and parks, but in their private possessions.

In many civilizations, for example in America or China, it is novelty, the latest things, whether a car, cell phone or piece of art that attracts favourable comment and perhaps envy. Many English visiting China are distressed to see swathes of beautiful old building being pulled down and replaced with identical tower blocks. And such visitors are also disappointed to find few junk or antique shops, though they may, if they are lucky enough to visit very rich homes, find wonderful old Chinese art.

The English keep their old furniture, ornaments, art works, sculpture and glassware. They delight in telling anyone who visits their homes about these family heirlooms or acquired objects. Their television shows, for example 'Antiques Roadshow', dealing with their old bits and pieces, are immensely popular. Many English attics and garages are filled with boxes of old objects which the family is reluctant to throw away. As Cammaerts remarks, 'This kind of box-room or lumber-room is not only characteristic of the English home but of all English institutions. There is a positive objection in England to anything that looks like "scrapping". Past traditions and titles and costumes are essentially respectable; they may have become useless, but if they do no good they can certainly do no harm, and then - who knows - there is an attractive element of doubt as to their future destinies.' [6]

Why this large difference exists between forward-looking and backward-looking civilizations would take a book to analyse. Yet some of the background – the long continuous history, mostly peaceful, with good conditions for preservation of objects, relative affluence, class-consciousness expressed in objects – is obvious. It is important to remember that 'old is good', 'new is suspect' in England.

If it has to be new in England, then it is a good idea to make it look as old as possible, as in neo-Gothic art. The English are masters of the 'invention of tradition'. Much of what seems old is, in fact, either re-invented, or newly invented with a surface of antiquity. One part of becoming a true native is to be able to tell the difference between real and fake antiquity.

Aplomb[7]

Aplomb, derived from the French *à plomb* meaning 'according to a plumb line' (a plumb line being a device to make buildings and other manufactures straight), is a word which offers another insight into English character. It means keeping steady under disturbance or challenges, remaining on course, being invariable. It is associated with self-confidence, especially in difficult situations. Other words which overlap with its meaning are self-assurance, self-possession, self-confidence, calmness, presence of mind, coolness, equilibrium, nonchalance. A frequent ingredient is humour, including self-mocking humour.

Many of the heroes of popular English books and films show this characteristic. In childrens' stories, Alice is full of it in Wonderland, Just William is full of it with his Outlaws, Bilbo Baggins is armed with it in his search for the Ring, Harry Potter shows it in his struggles against Voldemort. Aplomb is one of the central parts of the characters of James Bond, Dr Who and Ford Prefect in the *Hitchhiker's Guide to the Galaxy*.

The quality was central in British history, where the imperial rulers in distant lands were obeyed not so much out of fear, but through inspiring confidence with their aplomb attitude. Kipling celebrated at the very start of his widely popular 'If'.

> If you can keep your head when all about you
> Are losing theirs and blaming it on you,
> If you can trust yourself when all men doubt you,
> But make allowance for their doubting too;

Aplomb was the quality inculcated informally in the English educational system through games and informal activities, and now as I reflect on my own education, I see time and again that I was picking it up from all those around me.

After all, aplomb is not something you can consciously be taught. Rather, you learn it through observation and practice and often fall into it by accident. The self-confidence and humour comes first and then are expressed through meeting challenges with aplomb. Idries Shah, an acute Afghan observer of the English in his *Darkest England*, narrates how he accidentally fell into the ability to be aplomb.
At a diplomatic occasion in London he was approached by an Englishman.

'I say,' he said, 'are you from Trinidad?'

'No, actually,' I responded, 'are you?'

He looked at me for a moment: first in bewilderment and then with annoyance. 'Trinidad?' he snapped. 'I most certainly am NOT!'

Even the a British can be outwitted in the aplomb game by a visiting Afghan.

B

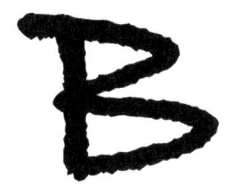

Barter

One of the shocks for the English when they go to much of the Middle East, India or China is to go to a market and to find that there are no set prices. The English are used to a world, which has clearly existed for at least a thousand years, where there is little or no bartering or haggling, processing which aim to force the buyer to raise his offer, or the seller to sell more cheaply. Instead, when you went to a shop or stall in England, or ordered goods, you asked how much it cost - and if you wanted it, you paid that. This is the world described by Adam Smith in his *Wealth of Nations* (1776) and it still largely exists.

This is very different from situations where the price of everything is elastic, a negotiable transaction depending on the social relationship of the individuals, the current needs and desires of the transactors at that precise moment in time, and the haggling skills of each.

The difference of approach reflects the difference between a highly regulated versus an irregular economy, a highly monetized economy as opposed to one where money only partially penetrates and social relations are dominant. It is the difference between societies where you would go to a fair or market where many dealers next to each other would be selling a range of identical goods, and the more specialized shop economy of England where, in a village, there might only be one baker, one butcher, one greengrocer. Here it was pointless to haggle. Other reasons were suggested by Count Pecchio when he observed 'In England there is no bargaining. The price of every article is fixed. This custom is not the product solely of competition and confidence, but also of the necessity of saving time.'[8]

The practical implication is that you should be careful when trying to barter in England. Shopkeepers and others may be open to lower offers, and this is particularly the case in open-air markets and at the end of the day. Yet in many contexts they would be surprised, even shocked, if you suggest that their prices are negotiable. It calls their skills and their honour into question. In short, you need to be careful if you intend to barter.

Beef

Although English restaurants and private homes are now quite cosmopolitan in the food they serve, some visitors find traditional English food dull and stodgy. The iconic dish was a slab of meat – roast beef – perhaps with Yorkshire pudding (a kind of pastry), and some over-boiled vegetables. There was a heavy meat content to much to the diet, and boiled vegetables, especially root vegetables like potatoes, carrots, swedes, beetroot and parsnips were much in evidence. The dishes had unappetising names, like 'toad in the hole' or 'bubble and squeak'. The puddings were often stodgy and over-sweet, with peculiar names such as 'spotted dick'. All this might be followed by rather hard cheese.

For those coming from rice or pasta-based cuisines, where vegetables were much more important and often cooked quickly in oil with spices, it all seems pretty unappetising.

The reasons behind these cuisine choices is quite obvious. The English have always had a very large pastoral, animal-filled, agriculture, producing copious amounts of meat (mutton from sheep, lamb, and beef from cows). They have had large amounts of milk to turn into butter and into forms of hard cheese which will last. These milk-based foods were inedible for many lactose-intolerant visitors. The English grew large amounts of root vegetables, both for themselves and their animals, in their rich soils, partly to rest their grain fields.

The Scots were equally unappetising in their foods: a stodgy breakfast of inferior grains (oats) made into porridge, traditionally eaten with salt, and their national dish, a sheep's stomach filled with the intestines of the animal (haggis).

Now it is much changed and visitors can eat the foods of the world, and even English food, especially the delicious fish and chips, can compete with any in the world.

Beer

Each nation has its national drink and this has many indirect effects on its character. Sake in Japan, whisky in Scotland and wine in France or Italy all shape and reflect certain characteristics. The connections are intriguing. For example, the areas where beer has been drunk are northern Germany, Holland, Scandinavia and England and these are exactly the areas where the Protestant form of Christianity flourished, while wine and Catholicism are synonymous.

Beer was widespread in England from the early sixteenth century, adding hops and hence anti-bacterial substances to keep the traditional drink of ale from going stale. The rich agriculture of England allowed the inhabitants to drink up to half of their grain harvest and led to improved health as the anti-bacterials in the beer and the absence of drinking contaminated water which was common in English.

Beer was traditionally made by small producers, often a widow or a poorer family. It thus improved the economic position of women. It was best drunk communally out of a barrel, and hence small drinking places, alehouses and pubs ('public' houses) abounded. Most English villages had many of these small communal drinking places, where neighbours would meet and where guests and travellers would meet and rest. The atmosphere was open, full of political and other discussion, a locus for friendship and informal alliances, a sort of club based around beer. Women often ran the small alehouses and sometimes the largest inns and frequented them in earlier centuries. It is very different from the continental coffee bar, traditionally only for men and for locals who have known each other for many years.

Any visitor to England will be well advised to explore this mild, not very intoxicating, healthful and sociable drink, to buy a round for the locals, and to chat to strangers. You will learn a lot by exploring the pubs and inns where, for centuries, much of English social, intellectual and local political life has been led, where detectives and scientists have also relaxed and solved their mysteries.

Brexit

This is a topic which will perhaps only be of historical interest in a few years. Currently, however, it is a great enigma and source of anxiety, not only for those observing the U.K. but even for the British themselves. We all ask, how did we get into this mess and how are we go get out of it?

The reasons for getting into this hole are both long term and immediate. Much of this little book explains the numerous and deep-seated historical and cultural differences between the U.K. and Europe. These have greatly lessened in the last two generations, but still many people sense that the English are very different in their traditions and culture from people across the Channel. This makes many people want to preserve the difference, the special law, the independent political power, the culture and identity. All these seem to be threatened by globalization. This leads to hostility and anxiety, not just in the U.K. but in many parts of the world at present.

A more immediate reason is that many who voted in the referendum to leave Europe were suffering an erosion of their lives by rapid technological changes, particularly automation and artificial intelligence. This compounded their feeling of hopelessness. Something different was offered by those who advocated withdrawal, a new world of opportunity and return to more satisfactory jobs, and many believed the promises. In this way, they were only doing what the British do every four years or so, voting against the current established party in power, throwing them out in the hope that the next lot would be better. This is what elective democracy is about.

Unfortunately, with hardly any experience of referenda, many did not fully realize that this was not a general election which, if it led to an unsatisfactory outcome, could be reversed. It was not a matter of changing the players at the top, but changing the fundamental rules of the game. It is like moving from cricket to football, not just choosing another coach or captain.

As the implication and full impact dawns, many believe that the pragmatic English are likely to find a way out of this tight corner. They have done so many times in their history. My guess in the spring of 2019 is that it is likely that Brexit will drift into a half in, half out, solution which is the usual answer to most problems - namely half way between the two extremes. The English hate all binary decisions and prefer something in-between. Compromise is central to an English person, constantly pulled in contrary directions by the divided world in which he or she lives.

Bribery

Bribery can be defined as the buying of favours. The buying does not have to be with money, and the favours can be of many kinds; permits or licence, political interventions, an educational qualification, the promotion of your close family. Bribery is, of course, universal and from our earliest childhood we are bribed by our parents and try to bribe them. It is often indirect: I teach your son, you get me a ticket to the opera. Without some bribery, all economic, social and political systems would quickly die.

There are, however, degrees of bribery and one of the contrasts is between relatively 'bribery-free' societies – Scandinavia, Holland, England spring to mind - and the vast majority. In the majority, many of the good things in life – health, wealth, education, political safety – can only be achieved by giving and receiving bribes.

The general term when extensive bribery is detected is 'corruption', which literally means the invasion of one entity by another, like rust eating up metal, or bacteria invading a healthy body or plant.

England for many centuries has been relatively bribery-free. It is neither necessary, and indeed counter-productive, to try to bribe officials, police, doctors, teachers and others. It is not sensible to try to bribe those in power – politicians and administrators. Even God, in the Protestant view, cannot be bribed by candles, incense or pilgrimages.

It is therefore wise to be very careful to avoid all hints of bribery in English life. Of course, you can exchange favours. You can help a friend or acquaintance or student or neighbour in one way and they return it in another. Yet even here you have to be a little careful. The rules are quite strict and the loss of reputation if you cross certain lines can be calamitous.

Bureaucracy

A bureau is a cabinet or desk with pigeon holes and shelves, in which the paper generated by an organization can be filed. It is the basis for the term 'bureaucracy', or, as my English grand-daughter put it when she was eight, 'bureau-crazy'.

Foreign observers in the eighteenth and nineteenth centuries have noted that the English seemed relatively free of bureaucracy. Bureaucracy meant the setting up of governmental and other organizations, staffed by paid and specially trained officials, who execute the commands of the government. They do this according to elaborate rule books and with the aim of making decisions through strict impartiality, the keeping to impersonal codes, making things explicit, and accounting to those above them in the organization.

I realized the difference when a visiting Japanese academic asked me where the rule book governing my life as a Cambridge academic could be consulted. He said that when he took on his job, a huge printed document was handed to him which he had to memorize. I replied that we did not have such a thing, in the same way that the English do not have a centre to their politics, in other words a written constitution. My instructions when I took up a life appointment as a University Lecturer, or when I became a Fellow of my College in Cambridge, consisted of two or three lines long, setting out my terms of contract.

This set me examining how most institutions in England have been organized and I realized that in all the professions, and in the government, work was largely based on custom, 'common sense', trust and freely given time and self-government. People who worked in the organization as teachers, doctors, lawyers, politicians, soldiers, were expected not only to do their professional job, but also to run their organization themselves with few or no paid official 'bureaucrats'. There is a downside to all this club atmosphere of course, for it can be used to keep out women, minorities, the young.

In the last thirty years the bureaucratization of all professions – education, medicine, law, local government – has increased hugely. Now it feels as if the English are drowning in bureaucracy in the pursuit of a nebulous transparency, equality and accountability. Yet shreds of the old trusting and commonsense system still remain and visitors may be surprised on occasion that they can do things without filling in elaborate forms or waiting interminably for 'faceless' bureaucrats. You may find people who are prepared to take personal responsibility and take decisions without referring to manuals, without checking with their superiors, without writing down carefully what has been decided in case there is future controversy.

C

Ceremony

It is not just in grand events, such as royal weddings and funerals, that the English show their love of ceremony. At many sporting, military or educational events, people dress up, make speeches, perform with elaborate walking and gestures. The ceremonial British used this type of behaviour to impress their subjects in India and the rest of the British Empire and they still enjoy ceremonial today.

Of course, all countries have ceremonies. Yet in most of them the primary reason is religious. There are pilgrimages with much devotional behaviour, the carrying of religious figures through the streets, pujas and Shinto celebrations. In these, the stylised costumes and gestures are believed to bring good fortune and health, to please the spirits. They are instrumental, done to gain some advantage.

What is unusual about the high degree of ceremonial activity in England is that it is not religious, but rather social – demonstrating power, class, the movement from one status (student, unmarried) to another (Master of Arts, married).

The individualism and huge differences between single persons and social groups in English society is, for a while, suspended in a choreographed unity. In these ceremonies, as in a formal dance, everyone takes their place and plays their part. For both the actors and the observers it gives a particularly absorbing satisfaction, a part of being something larger than themselves, a kind of team game of another kind.

Christmas

Each civilization has its central ceremonial focal point, the occasion when a family unites to celebrate, usually in some semi-religious way, their unity. Hindu societies have Holi, Tihar, Dasain in the Spring and Autumn, which is also when the Chinese have their two main festivals. In both these cases and many others, the festival often brings together dozens of relatives and lasts for days and perhaps several weeks.

The English have taken the birth of their incarnate God, Jesus, as their central festival. This is celebrated all over the Christian world, but the English have given it a local colouring. Because the family is often widely dispersed once the children are grown up, and more distant relatives are relatively unimportant, Christmas is at its most intense when parents still live with their young children in the house.

The filling of the stockings with presents and later the Christmas (fir) tree surrounded with presents is special. There are myths told of Father Christmas and his reindeer and children believe, and then, reluctantly, half-believe, these stories. There is special food and drink and the day after, when boxes or presents were given to tradesmen in the past and hence known as Boxing Day, may continue the celebrations with leftovers from the previous day and a bracing walk or, in some places, animal hunt.

Christmas for the English often only lasts two or three days. It is usually a rather private affair and it is a singular sign of friendship to be invited to an English family to share their Christmas. For many it can be a time of stress, balancing the demands of different parts of the family and perhaps creating a slightly false sense of harmony to cover over the tensions which have arisen during the year, or been avoided by living well apart. It is also a great consumer spree, for some a moment of nostalgia or spiritual excitement, for children a taste of magic, and for a nation as it sits watching its old classic films or watching the choir of King's College Cambridge singing Christmas carols, the coming together of an invisible, imagined, community of the nation – here and all over the world.

Cleanliness

Dirt, as a well-known Victorian English proverb put it, is 'matter out of place'. Most things are fine in a certain position – horse manure on a field, human manure in a toilet, outdoor shoes in the hallway, but if they are put in another area, cross a certain invisible boundary, they become 'dirt' and people will react with disgust and sometimes feel physically sick.

In the past, it was generally reckoned that the Japanese were ultra-clean and even to this day there is an almost obsessive attention both in public and in the home to cleanliness. Not a used match is left for long on a subway platform and it is deeply disgusting to wear outdoor shoes into a house. The Dutch were thought to be the most cleanly in Europe, with the scrubbed houses shown in Dutch paintings. Then came the English who took considerable trouble, though their streets filled with horses and their heavy furniture and fittings let them down.

As for other peoples of the world apart from the Japanese, by English or Dutch standards historically they lacked cleanliness. It was often a criticism of Indians, Chinese and even Mediterranean peoples that they suffered dirt to lie around. Perhaps they were too poor to have the time and energy to clean up. Yet it seemed more than this, for they did not seem to notice the filth that upset certain travellers.

All this has changed and much of China, for example, is now spotless and puts the English to shame. Nevertheless, it is worth being careful to find out about the dirt codes of the U.K. No littering in the streets and fields, dog excrement carefully collected up in little plastic bags and safely disposed of, not throwing rubbish out of cars or windows, when and where to wear your shoes. 'Cleanliness is next to Godliness', is an old English saying and clean habits are much commended.

Cliques[9]

A clique is a small sub-group or circle of people who exclude others from membership of their group. Visitors or temporary residents in a new country often sense that they are shut out of many such sub-groups, or from the culture as a whole, though the degree to which this is a problem varies greatly from country to country.

Going to Japan, you meet great kindness and courtesy, but it is unlikely that you will be absorbed, invited into private homes, or become 'Japanese', however long you stay in the country, learn the language or even marry locally. In contrast, going to a Nepalese village, I was quickly absorbed and soon had been adopted into two families, thus calling many people by kinship terms. When my 'mother' died, I was one of the four closest relatives who were asked to light the ritual funeral pyre.

Colleagues who have worked on the European Continent have often found it very difficult to penetrate inside private homes and Arthur Koestler the writer relates how, during several years working in Paris, he never felt close to anyone or was asked into a French home. Immediately he came to England, he was absorbed into people's families and homes.

Yet, despite this, some of my Chinese friends say that they find the English put up invisible barriers. A friendship seems to start, even visiting a home for a meal, but it never develops further. They are disappointed.

The secret to overcoming this was put by C.S. Lewis the writer when he wrote 'The English do not have friends. They have friends *about* things.' In other words, just being happy together and chatting is not enough. You need something more to bond you.

As individualistic and often quite reserved, as well as being busy in many spheres, the one way to make and continue a deeper friendship in England is to find a common interest, a shared hobby, passion, project, or even a club. If there is not a mutual 'game' to play, then the relationship will falter. This is true even in English companionate (based on equal companionship) marriage, where the strongest marriages are those where husband and wife share some kind of mutual project to which they contribute. If they do not do so, it is easy for them to have nothing to talk about and to drift apart.

So, if you like someone in England, find something you want to do together, something creative to build on or play together at. This will give you a chance to explore each other's worlds and to be constantly refreshed with new thoughts and experiences in your relationship. You may form your own clique, but at least you will not feel excluded.

Clubs

An unusual institution cross-culturally, yet a vital part of the English system is the club. In most civilizations, people's lives are organized by, and they associate mainly with family or village neighbours. The kin group owns property together, worships together, enjoys leisure time and pursues political power as a group. Blood and marriage are the principles for forming into effective groups, and sometimes religion as in caste societies.

We have seen that kinship is fragmented and people are separated in English society. Yet people still need to unite for many purposes – to enjoy leisure, to discuss and solve problems, to pursue political or economic power more effectively. Historically at least, the English achieved this mostly through clubs.

A club is a private, non-state, organization set up by a small group of usually non-family-related people who have a particular purpose in mind. They may want to play cricket or golf or football, to encourage economic co-operation in trade or manufacturing, to make music, to pursue literary or scientific co-operation, or to influence the religious or political situation.

The club sets up a body which makes rules and owns property (a club house of some kind with appropriate club amenities such as a library, sitting room, bar). It is managed by a committee and elects and ejects members by popular vote. England and America are full of clubs of dozens of kinds and such institutions are the basis for their civil society.

Anyone staying in the U.K. for a while should investigate what clubs are open to them in their field of interest, talk to some members, get elected and enjoy a particularly English form of sociality and mutual support.

Coal[10]

Like tea, coal is in the blood of the English (and Scots and Welsh of course). One of the greatest breakthroughs in world history, the industrial revolution pioneered in England from the 1780s, was based on coal. Some have even suggested that the drab blacks and greys of English towns and traditional costumes is somehow linked to the all-pervasive black dust and huge piles of coal. Coal created the mines, the canals, the factories and was the fuel of the huge British Empire. Now that the coal age has disappeared for over fifty years, it is difficult to remember how much British culture revolved around coal.

It is easy to assume that coal only became important for the English around the mid eighteenth century. In fact, coal was mined fourteen hundred years ago and by about eight hundred years ago it was important as a source of heat and for making the lime to fertilize the fields. By four hundred years ago, a century before the industrial revolution, a great deal of British energy needs were supplied by coal and coal saved the remaining forests from being destroyed for fuel, encouraged a large shipping trade along the coasts and helped the growth of London.

At a deeper level, the presence of this fossil fuel encouraged the British to develop a machine-based civilization, to value the replacement of human labour by alternative forms of energy alongside wind and water. Without coal, England would be a very different country today. It would have in all probability remained a small, unimportant, island off the western tip of Europe, probably colonized by one of the continental countries.

Common sense

The idea of 'common sense' plays a considerable part in all aspects of English life. In the law courts it takes the form of 'the reasonable man' (or woman), the index for judging if someone is lying, and also for allocating blame if someone behaves 'unreasonably'. In politics, the family, the commercial world, and even in science, it often comes down to doing what 'common sense' suggests.

It was at times assumed by the English that all humans around the world would look at things in the same way, applying 'common sense' to problems. Yet cross-comparatively I know of few places where such a concept is important, for various reasons.

To start with, there is no such thing as 'common'. Sense for a peasant is different from sense for a lord, for a worker different from that of the boss, for a woman different from that for a man, for a child different from an adult, for a lower caste from an upper caste, for a Hindu different from a Muslim. The assumption that anyone you meet will have the same common, or in-common views, ethics, desires and logic as yourself is an extraordinary one, even if it tends to be strongest when people are of the same class, gender and schooling.

There is also the question of what constitutes 'sense', and its opposite, nonsense. Sense is not something you can be taught formally in schools, but rather a habit or set of customary rules which an English person is expected to pick up as they grow. They will learn from those around them that this 'makes sense' and that is nonsense. They will learn of precedents and previous solutions. People gain in sense early on, and even children of a few years old are assumed to have a good common sense.

Good sense is usually based on a balance between opposites, a middle of the road, pragmatic, resolution to the constant tensions and ambiguities of life. It is the opposite of illogicality (nonsense), of over-enthusiastic zealotry and intolerance.

Any visitor to England should develop both a reverence for this commendable quality, and the skill to practice common sense. Once you have it, you can sway others to see the common sense of your particular view.

Communities

Most people in most civilizations through history have grown up in a community. Such a community is a group of people united by three things, blood or family relations, a defined space where they were born and will live all their lives, and a name or identity, 'We, the...'

Great peasant civilisations such as China, Russia, India, the Mediterranean and east European nations and South and Middle America were based on communities. Even when the people move into cities, communities tended to form.

An examination of English history shows that there has never been anything equivalent to this. The Anglo-Saxons were tribal peoples who did not either in their laws or customs set up strong communities. Such communities have been absent as a concept in England since then. Even in the most isolated period of rural communities, the nineteenth and first half of the twentieth century, with the depopulation of the countryside, classic works such as

Rev. J.C. Atkinson's *Forty Years in Moorland Parish* (1891), or Flora Thompson's *Lark Rise to Candleford* (1939 on), give a different feeling to that which we find in accounts of French, Italian, let alone Chinese or Indian, villages.

England is based not on Community (*gemeinschaft*), but on Association (*gesellschaft*). This difference, one of the deepest oddities of the English, needs to be understood if much else is to make sense. English life is based on freely entered into, implicitly contractual, relationships, which enable people to set up their own networks and constantly adapt them through friendship and collaboration. Most societies in history have been based on birth-given and permanent relationships, based on the relative status of family, age and gender, and often caste, which people cannot alter. This all makes a huge difference to the feel of a civilization.

Crime

The patterns of crime in each civilization mirror both in their nature and quantity the values of that civilization. The Japanese, and to a considerable extent the Chinese, have had and still have low crime rates. This is explained by many things, including the system of mutual responsibility and punishment, and very severe collective punishment in the past. Individualistic and affluent societies in the West often have high crime rates and, in some cases, for example in America, with very high rates of gun-crime, a great deal of violence.

The English traditionally had middling levels of crime. The crimes were mainly centred on what one might call 'capitalist' or money-centred offences – burglary (entering a person's house), robbery (attacking people outside their homes), and the various species of 'white collar' crimes such as bank fraud or tinkering with the currency ('coining and clipping').

Where all kinds of collective grouping except the family are suppressed, and where the family is very strong, there emerge strong criminal gangs and much crime is done by them, based on family-like honour – the Mafia, Triads and Yakuza. Such organizations were largely absent until very recently in England, though they are now emerging. Crime was, like much else, mainly individualistic, or perhaps, as with highway robbery, involved small and fluctuating gangs of non-related accomplices. There were highway robbers, occasional semi-bandits represented by the fictional Robin Hood and his Merry Men. Yet normally, most crime was carried out by the lone individual.

On the whole, it is still the case that England is fairly safe from crime. Despite periodic panics about terrorism, knife crimes or acid attacks, you can mostly walk the streets and live without fear in most of England. Yet it is wise to keep things locked up since random thefts are possible. Another thing to look out for is that by a quirk of the English law of trespass, a stranger can enter and stay in your house legally, as long as he or she has not forced an entry or done any damage. Hence 'squatting' or occupying unused premises becomes common at times, and certain groups, for example gypsies, make use of the ambiguity of the law to settle temporarily on unoccupied land.

D

Decency[11]

What is decent, that is to say in particular which parts of the human body can be shown to which others in which contexts, is hugely variable. Some westerners were shocked to find the topless African or Pacific islanders. Yet foreigners were often shocked to find English women without hats on special occasions, or wearing clinging or low-cut dresses.

There are many paradoxes here. Traditionally the Japanese practiced mixed naked bathing, yet Japanese girls were deeply shocked if a foreign male offered to help them over a stile. The English usually covered over most of their bodies, but also delighted in naked bathing (there were famous naked bathing places on the river just outside both Oxford and Cambridge for example).

Nowadays, of course, the codes are immensely complex. The presence of many groups in the U.K., for example those who adhere to stricter forms of Islam, mean that we are very aware that any part of the body, the hair, lips, feet, may be considered an area which needs covering.

Again, the only way through this maze is to consult and observe the local inhabitants. The situation is medium relaxed and starting with the normal clothing of China, or the universal jeans and jerseys, is usually safe. Yet you may still get the occasional shock, as I have had in both China and Japan. A particular case is that in both, male and female toilets sometimes overlap to an extent that women have to pass urinating men. Indecency is considered a fairly serious offence against good manners in English, though people are usually too polite to be openly critical. Yet it is good to be aware.

Eating[12]

The behaviour surrounding one of the most central of human activities, eating food, is filled with hidden rules and customs. There is the question of what you use to eat with and how you do so. There are three great bands of methods. The Far East eats with chop-sticks and there are many rules about these, for example you should not use your personal chop-sticks to pick food from small bowls of food, except in certain situations.

The middle band of Burma, India, Pakistan and Sri Lanka, is one where almost everyone eats with their hands. Again, there are rules, for example you should wash your hands before and after eating and you should never eat with your left hand.

Then there is the western, knife and fork, band within which England is included. Again, things like how you arrange your knife and fork after you finish eating, how you hold them, what you put on your knife and many other rules are relevant. Eating properly was something which my schools paid close attention to.

Then there is the order of eating. In more elaborate meals, the English usually start with a savoury course - often soup. Then there is a main meat dish (or in more elaborate meals, fish then meat), then a pudding or sweet dish, finally perhaps cheese and biscuits and fruit. It is polite to finish all the food on your plate, therefore advisable not to take too much at first, but add to it with a second helping. Do not help yourself without asking permission, but asking for a second helping is also a compliment to the cook.

You should express pleasure and congratulations on the food, ask after the recipe, note special high points. You should, when dining privately, not expect to take away left-overs (a 'doggy bag' as it used to be called). Nor should you, as in some cultures, express satisfaction by belching - that would be extremely rude.

You should eat moderately quickly. The English, like the Japanese, tend to think of eating as a necessity, but it is not the centre of their life and should be finished reasonably fast in order to get to more important things.

Education

In terms of the relation of the school to the family, and the role of the school in relation to the pupil, the aim of English education is unusual. When the child went to school, he or she was being taken out of, away from, the family. The school acted in place of the parents, *in loco parentis* as is said in Latin, in other words the school *became* the parents.

The teachers and the other children created a parallel world to the home, where friendship and mentoring meant that the child learnt most of the skills and morals for adult life. Here children learnt the social skills – how to survive pressures, how to make friends, how to concentrate and experiment. Here they learnt the private political skills – how to obey and how to command, how to manoeuvre and how to plot. Here they learnt the basics of their spiritual and moral existence since all schools until recently were directly or indirectly linked to the Christian Church. Here they learnt the laws of the market through hobbies and games that taught them the laws of supply and demand, bargaining, co-operation and competition.

Put in another way, the role of the schools in England was to take a young child of about eight and shape, mould, prune them, not just their mind, but also their personality and character, their spirit and their emotions, as well as their bodies.

This total role of schools was seen at its most extreme in the form of boarding schools which took children away from home, first to 'preparatory schools' (preparing for the next stage) from eight to thirteen, and then to 'public schools' from thirteen to eighteen. This was then rounded off by the universities, which had previously taken much younger students from the age of fourteen or fifteen, but by the nineteenth century were dealing with the present age range.

Yet the system was not restricted to private schools. The idea that schools are the essential transit mechanism for many children away from the family and into society can be seen in the grammar schools and even in nursery and kindergarten. In each case the school provides a sheltered environment, a place for social transition. This is unique.

This means that when we examine English schooling, we see that it is designed to provide a *generic* training for individuals who might, with the array of social ladders and professions, end up in all sorts of job – banker, soldier, lawyer, merchant, clergyman, teacher.

In England education is the mechanism which keeps the system open, flexible, ever changing, yet also maintains certain traditions and myths. It is also the main bulwark of the class system. It is often harsh, often painful, but certainly, in its own way, rather extraordinary.

Equality

George Orwell wrote that 'The whole English-speaking world is haunted by the idea of human equality, and though it would be simply a lie to say that either we or the Americans have ever acted up to our professions, still, the idea is there, and it is capable of one day becoming a reality'[13]. Orwell also caught the paradox arising from the English belief that all humans are intrinsically equal, yet in practice they end up unequal in a system which also values liberty, a free market and the capitalist system, in his famous (adapted) statement 'All men are equal, but some are more equal than others'.

There is a basic assumption of equality in English civilization. It is and has long been assumed that people are born equal and free in the sight of God and the Law and they can make their way as they think best. Yet everyone knows that the dice are loaded. Chance, birth position, class, the many events of their lives, means that this basic equality of opportunity is converted over a lifetime into a society where there are often gross inequality, with the poorest in England today liable to die on average ten years or more earlier than the rich.

Yet, despite the failures and the inequalities, it is worth being aware that unlike almost every other civilization on earth, the English believe in the premise of equality, and not in the premise of innate inequality. This means that however poor, weak, young old, black, brown or white you are, you should be treated, and treat others, as essentially an equal human being. We are equal in the sight of God, the tax man and the judge, even if some are clearly more fortunate than others.

Ethics

There is something contradictory about English ethics. On the one hand, ethics plays a much larger part in English life, and particularly in the area we designate as 'religion', than in many societies. English religion, Taine wrote 'subordinates ritual and dogma to ethics'.[14] The puritan conscience is well known, highly concerned with ethics, and it is clear that this conscience is a continuation of an earlier cultural feature. Self-examination and concern with 'doing the right thing', including a sense of guilt, is a very old feature of English history. One can argue that the English, and those they have influenced, particularly in the settlement of New England, are the most ethically earnest of peoples.

On the other hand, it can be argued that the ethical system is quite weak because of the conflicting demands of a highly separated world. There are few over-arching imperatives and no absolutes. Such absolutes are possible in a society where some institution, whether religion or the family, is all powerful. Yet where people live in a constant pull from different forces there is no clear ethical line to be followed.

The English are aware of the dangers of the love of money and greed, yet are full of the desire for wealth. They are aware of the dangers of lust, yet have had a relatively relaxed sexual code. They are aware of the dangers of selfishness, yet are taught to be very self-contained, self-reliant and even self-centred. They are hesitant, conflicted, caught in endless ethical and philosophical dilemmas, brilliantly put by one of their great poets, Alexander Pope, in his 'Essay on Man' (Epistle II), which might, more appropriately, have been titled 'Essay on the English Man (and Woman)'.

> He hangs between; in doubt to act, or rest;
> In doubt to deem himself a god, or beast;
> In doubt his mind or body to prefer;

> Born but to die, and reas'ning but to err;
> Alike in ignorance, his reason such,
> Whether he thinks too little, or too much:
> Chaos of thought and passion, all confus'd;
> Still by himself abus'd, or disabus'd;
> Created half to rise, and half to fall;
> Great lord of all things, yet a prey to all;
> Sole judge of truth, in endless error hurl'd:
> The glory, jest, and riddle of the world!

Etiquette[15]

Etiquette is basically the complex sphere of inter-personal behaviour in various contexts. You have the etiquette of eating, drinking, walking through doorways and along crowded streets and of driving cars.

Because England was and is a constantly shifting class society, etiquette along with language was a main marker of class and quickly revealed a person's position on the class ladder. There are many books on English etiquette, and quite a bit of attention was paid to various aspects of this in my boarding school education.

It is difficult in a few words to give much advice on the subject, but here are a few of the basic rules I learnt.

Always show that you are aware of the other and hold them in respect. This applies particularly in relation to the opposite sex, the old and the infirm. Thus, opening the door for them, helping them in difficult situations, being attentive so that they do not need to ask for things, all are signs of good breeding.

Treating people with courtesy and not making demands or taking their actions for granted involves using the words 'Please' and 'Thank you' very often, even to people close to you such as your spouse, children, parents, and certainly with all those you meet or work with.

Etiquette applies to everyone, not just to your superiors or equals. You should not be fawning and obsequious to richer or more powerful people, but treat them with the same respect you treat others with. Nor should you ever be rude or treat with disrespect or arrogance people who are currently weaker, poorer, less well educated than yourself. This applies particularly to people who are in a serving position – servants, porters or bus drivers.

Etiquette basically means making an effort on behalf of another person, taking time and trouble to put them before yourself, showing that you are aware of their inner thoughts and needs. Etiquette preserves your honour and enhances that of the other. It is a kind of personal gift in the form of words and actions, which decreases the frictions of life and it has to be shown constantly and in all situations and relations.

Evil

The ambivalence of the English towards the idea of Evil mirrors many of their other contradictions. On the one hand, as descendants of a Christian society, they have internalized a binary image of God and the Devil, the idea that there are certain things which are entirely black, others that are entirely white. Their Lord's Prayer asked to be 'delivered from All Evil'. They constantly talk about this or that, for example the latest terrorist atrocity, the bombing of another city, even the doings of a politician they dislike, as 'utterly Evil'. Hitler, Stalin, Pol Pot are Evil monsters and the many accidents and abuses of life are Evil. The English seem to be confident that they know Evil when they see it.

Yet their sense of Evil is so watered down that it is probably more appropriate to use the word with a small initial letter, evil, and to see it as normally meaning 'very very bad' or ethically unacceptable, or something that shocks us. Thus, you can use the word evil about wasting food or ruining the environment, or sexual abuse, or the evils of capitalism or communism. It is just saying that one strongly disapproves of something.

This watering down seems to be related to the saying 'The love of money is the root of all evil'. In a capitalist society, evil becomes good, good evil. Karl Marx quoted Shakespeare approvingly because he had seen this central feature.[16] A passage from Timon of Athens (Act IV, scene 3) is worth quoting at greater length than that in Marx's work. Timon digs in the ground and finds gold.

Gold? yellow, glittering precious gold? ...
Thus much of this will make black, white; foul, fair;

> Wrong, right; base, noble; old, young, coward, valiant.
> Ha, you gods! why this? What this, you gods? Why, this
> Will lug your priests and servants from your sides;
> Pluck stout men's pillows from below their heads:
> This yellow slave
> Will knit and break religions; bless the accurs'd;
> Make the hoar leprosy ador'd; place thieves,
> And give them title, knee, and approbation,
> With senators on the bench: ...

In other words, gold transforms everything, from black to white and back again; it brings together as equivalents things that are not really on the same plane and divides things that are naturally together. Man is no longer able to discriminate between what is good, and what is evil. It is a morally relativistic world where Good can easily turn into Evil, and the reverse. Evil is in the eye of the beholder, not in the thing which he or she looks at.

F

Fair play

A Chinese acquaintance who had been in England for eighteen years asked me with puzzlement what the English mean by 'Fair Play', which seems so important in many parts of their life. I answered that it is based on the idea that much of life is a rules-regulated game, whether in politics, the economic market, the law or the family.

In such a game, the players know the rules and they also know that they can be broken to their advantage without a referee or umpire noticing, or perhaps being able to do anything about it. There are a thousand tricks and deceits that you can use to gain your short-term advantage. If all else fails, you can bribe or threaten the referee.

Those who play fairly are those who do not break either the letter or the spirit of the rules. They are guided by an inner conscience which urges them to deal with the other in a way that does not take advantage of their temporary weakness or the absence of the referee. They are encouraged to put the long-term good of the whole team, and of the game as a game, above their narrow self-interest.

In most countries, though most of history, such fair play would be taken as a sign of weakness, or of foolishness, or of betrayal of your family or other group. The rules of the system are believed to be unfair and biased against you, and to play fairly within them will get you nowhere and only perpetuate your disadvantage.

To forgo a chance for personal and family advantage in pursuit of some abstract notion of fair play is often considered naive at the best, insane at the worst. The English who do so, and seem to assume that those they meet around the world will do the same, are clearly insane – perhaps affected by too much sunlight; as the song goes, 'Mad Dogs and English Men go out in the mid-day sun'.

Fishing and hunting

It has often been observed that the English have been obsessed with pursuing animals –fish, birds and mammals, particularly foxes and deer. Though this is now less central to their way of life, such activities are still important and the way in which they do this and what animals they pursue tells us a lot about the society.

The fact that the English have for many centuries had enough leisure, and enough protected rivers and land on which to practice what used to be called 'huntin, shootin, fishin', is a significant indication of their considerable wealth and their protected private property.

These sports, like games, appeal to the English as a way of relaxing, of retreating into a kind of meditative state, completely absorbed for a while and suspending all other worries and the pressures of social relations. Here they have a similar function to the huge obsession with the tea ceremony in some parts of the world, or the bagatelle-like game of *pachinko* in Japan, calligraphy or archery in traditional China.

This calming function helps to explain why fishing for 'coarse' (that is inedible) fish was until recently the most popular hobby in the U.K. where millions would go down at the week-end and sit by still water watching a float. If they caught anything they would put it back alive.

On the other hand, the upper middle classes would pursue more exciting 'game' creatures, often paying a lot for the sport. They would fish for trout and salmon, shoot pheasants and grouse, hunt foxes or deer. This was a class marker and if a rich visitor wants to impress his rich English friend he or she should learn their skills. If there is sufficient money, then buying a stretch of salmon river or grouse moor is likely to impress certain people. Watching the English as they ply their rods and guns is a study in national character.

Folk Culture

I remember an academic friend of mine coming back from a tour of the great museums of popular folk culture on the Continent, in France, Portugal, Italy and Austria, and bemoaning the fact that there seemed to be nothing like them in England. He suggested we should try to launch a proper Folk Museum. I tried to explain to him that it was impossible, for the simple reason that the English never had a 'Folk' or *Volk* as it is in German.

The reason for this absence is quite simple. In all the Continental nations, as in China or India or South America, there is a huge opposition between the High, literate, urban, culture of the few, and the Low, popular, unwritten folk culture of the masses. Anthropologists term this the opposition between the Great and the Little traditions.

The houses, tools, clothes, rituals, stories, in fact everything in material and non-material culture is different between these two segments. For example, the French and Germans and Celts have great collections of 'folk' stories and 'folk' music (as opposed to urban, civilized, 'high', written traditions), but the English do not.

If you go to a 'Folk' museum such as that in Cambridge, you will find it is in fact a class museum. It is filled with nineteenth and early twentieth century objects made and used by the working and lower middle class, often mass produced and factory made. Or if you examine English 'folk' customs, for example the Morris dance, you find they were invented in the seventeenth century or later, the same century in which a number of children's folk games and songs, for example 'Ring a ring of roses, a pocket full of posies', referring to the Plague in 1665, were also constructed.

English 'folk' museums are those of foreign 'folk', the Victoria and Albert Museum's Asian collections, the Museum of Mankind, the anthropology museums of Oxford and Cambridge and Manchester. They are certainly worth visiting, but they tell you of the British Empire, not of any separate medieval English peasant past.

Footpaths and parks

One of our great surprises on visits to Japan or China or even southern France was to find that it was very difficult to walk, that is to find a path which links to other paths, bridle-ways, green lanes, drove roads, and a mass of 'rights of way' across private land which anyone can use if they behave sensibly. Even in America, where it is often thought bizarre to walk anywhere where a car can drive, except in national parks, the ubiquitous English footpath, from a single thin strip to a broad grass highway, is rare.

These 'rights of way' are often of Anglo-Saxon and medieval origin and cover the whole country – even extending to a considerable extent into cities. When they consolidate into a mass they become a public park, criss-crossed with paths and with ponds, benches, flower-beds. Both paths and parks are unusual cross-comparatively outside Britain and depend on a concept of property, namely that different kinds of right can exist simultaneously and many things that are 'public', such as parks and footpaths, can be enjoyed under certain conditions by the wider public.

The enjoyment is hedged in with rules. You should not damage or appropriate the amenity in any way. You should shut gates behind you, keep dogs on leads, refrain from picking flowers or fruit, not light a fire or put up a tent. Yet as long as you keep sauntering or sitting, don't damage the fields, flowers or trees, there are thousands of miles of wonderful English countryside to explore. It is a treasure not to be found anywhere else in the world, even if it is constantly under threat.

Foreigners

There is a rather delightful story told of an English lady on the Rhine who, 'on hearing a German speaking of her party as foreigners, exclaimed, "No, we are not foreigners; we are English; it is you that are foreigners".' [17] This indicates one aspect of the traditional attitude of the English towards 'foreigners' – a too-common sublime arrogance. Reading accounts of the British and their Empire, one often senses that such a view was writ large, that the Indians in India, for example, were sometimes regarded as the real foreigners in their own land, there on sufferance of the British whose home it really was.

This is all very curious since the English themselves, of course, are all foreigners in England. They descend from wave after wave of migration – Anglo-Saxon, Vikings, Norman, French, Dutch and many more since. Yet, as still happens, as the new wave settles and is absorbed, it sees itself as native. Myths and rituals are invented to make it seem as if it has always been around.

In many ways, this is a healing process and melting into the

English is far better, most would think, than setting up ghettoes. It is also remarkable that many parts of England are now so multi-ethnic that people have ceased even to notice major differences of colour or creed.

Yet it is still worth remembering the old arrogance. If you are treated in a derogatory way you can inwardly smile to yourself and recognize that people who live in corners, as the saying goes, tend to think of themselves as special and wish to emphasize difference. Remember that the person who is treating you in this way is probably the son or grandson, or certainly descended from, foreigners. Few have put this thought better than Daniel Defoe in his poem 'The True Born Englishman' of the late seventeenth century, part of which reads.

> 'A true-born Englishman's a contradiction,
> In speech an irony, in fact a fiction.
> ...
> 'Tis well that virtue gives nobility,
> How shall we else the want of birth and blood supply?
> Since scarce one family is left alive,
> Which does not from some foreigner derive.'

Fourth estate

One of the major contributions of the English to world civilization is in the field of journalism, writing for papers, magazines, or commenting on radio and television. Newspapers began to be circulated in bulk in England from the seventeenth century and from then on, many famous papers such as *The Times*, *The Manchester Guardian*, *The Telegraph*, *Punch* and many others have been produced. The papers and journals travelled around the world.

The journalists kept the English united and focused on politics, society and sport through the great period of empire and then adapted into the vastly influential radio and television journalism, most famously in the British Broadcasting Corporation or B.B.C.

The richness of this journalistic tradition can be explained by several factors. There is the relative press freedom, only matched in England's former colony, the United States. Almost everywhere, until very recently, journalists were tightly controlled by the State, as they still are in over half of the world today.

Then there is the very large market for journalistic products created by an unusually large, wealthy, literate and fairly leisurely middle class. This is added to by the language which is, in the hands of a journalist such as George Orwell and many others, tough, direct, highly flexible, yet also full of double meanings.

The effect has been that democracy is strengthened by what is called The Fourth Estate. The term comes from the traditional European concept of the three estates of the realm, the clergy, nobility and commoners. To these can now be added a fourth, more informal, centre of power, namely the news media or press. This fourth estate has, among its functions, the critique of power and the holding of people to account.

Journalists educate and inform. When journalism dies, either through direct attacks and censorship, or through apathy or distraction by trivia and hedonism, democracy dies too. In England democracy and journalism are linked at a fundamental level.

When we visit China or Japan or any other country, we read the local papers and watch the local television. If you want to understand the English, read their journals and watch their more serious television programmes. Or, now that their journalism has spread all over the world, you can watch CNN or Al Jazeera.

Gentlemen

A Japanese friend once pointed out to me that there is something odd about England in the huge power of the upper middle class, the gentry level. In Japan he said, the power lay further down with the salary men and factory workers. In most traditional civilisations it has been at the top amongst the very rich nobility. Yet in England, both in central and local government, it is the gentry class that has dominated society.

The very word 'gentleman' was difficult to understand and many foreign observers were puzzled. It did not seem to be based on blood and birth, nor was it a legal status. Rather it was a matter of breeding (education) and a certain level of wealth. The gentleman had no privileges in law. It seemed to be based entirely on how you behaved and the status lay in the eyes of the beholder. You were a gentleman if people esteemed you as such.

Others would count you a gentleman (or lady) if you had the appropriate accent, house, furniture, education and leisure activities. Yet above all, it was your attitudes and behaviour that mattered. Rich men with all the material trappings and even the accent and education might not be gentlemen if they did not abide by the code of honour, trustworthiness, willingness to take on public, unpaid, service for a society. The top schools and universities' main function was to instill this gentlemanly code and spirit, which could not be bought directly with money. On the other hand, working class people could be 'nature's gentlemen', but only with a certain amount of leisure and wealth was it possible to be a 'gentleman' in the fullest sense.

Gifts

The giving of gifts is a very important part of social life but hugely variable. It is so important because gifts are not just physical objects, but embody social relationships and in particular contain a 'spirit' or element which requires that most gifts be returned or reciprocated in some way. As the English put it 'There is no such thing as a free lunch', in other words even when a lunch is paid for by another, there is some implied reciprocal favour in it.

To whom, when, what and how the gift is presented are an endless source of interest. Particularly important is whether the gift is given before the reciprocal favour is expected – when it becomes instrumental and can easily be read as a bribe, or after the favour, when it is expressive, and a kindness.

Gift-giving between members of a family, between workers and their bosses, to strangers, seems to be much more emphasized in Asian societies than in England. The Japanese are famous for their 'wrapping culture', exquisitely wrapped gifts which the recipient should not open until the giver has gone. The Chinese shower one with wonderful gifts – usually tea, art-works, scarfs and calligraphy. They traditionally present gifts of money in red packets to bosses and family at festivals, though some of this is currently discouraged as close to bribery.

Coming from such gift-giving cultures it is important to know that the English are a little suspicious of gift-giving, wondering what is behind the gift. If it is an expression of thanks for time and attention already given, it will be gladly and gratefully received. Yet if it is unsolicited, rather valuable, from someone one suspects wants something from you, then it can cause friction.

The best course is probably, if you want to give gifts, to give something of symbolic, but little monetary value, a picture of your home town, a small book of poetry in translation, a nice book mark. Basically, there is little expectation of gifts – friendship, kindness, interest, are the best gifts which the English can receive, or give.

Green[18]

Visitors to England whom I have asked about their strongest impression when arriving, have often said 'How green it is'. I get this shock also when I return from India or China. Yet after a few weeks I tend to take the greenness for granted, until on a summer day, or walking through a wood, I am suddenly struck by it again. Once you think about it, despite the fact that it is one of the most densely-packed countries on the planet, with large cities and many motorways, England remains very green.

Partly, of course, it is the climate. Large parts of the world are brown and denuded, covered in snow or deserts. Very few have reasonable temperate rainfall. Partly it is the soil, for example English grass meadows are impossible in Japan, even with constant watering, because the volcanic ash is not suitable for grass, and only in Hokkaido can you seriously raise cattle.

It may also be related in some way to the fact that the eyes of those in the far East, often leading to early-onset myopia, pick up the red and gold end of the spectrum best, while European, including British, eyes pick up the blue-green end. So, the English particularly love green in their gardens, while Chinese or Japanese gardens often have gold and red pavilions in them.

Yet it is more than this, or rather it is a circular process. The good grass allowed a very large animal-based agriculture, sheep in the Cotswold's, northern England and East Anglia, cows elsewhere. Consequently, there were many meadows and open grasslands. The private estates and the need for oak and other trees, as well as private hunting, preserved the forests.

The English love of green led to the parks and private gardens with their lawns, which turned even their cities, and now their motorway verges, green. 'Greensleeves' is one of their favourites traditional melodies, although the words and melody probably came originally from Italy, and they love to sing William Blake's song on Jerusalem, which imagines the city being rebuilt 'in England's green and pleasant land', cleared of the 'dark Satanic mills' of industrialism.

Greetings and gestures

The way in which you first greet another can make a huge difference to a future relationship, and the ways in which this is done tells us a good deal about a society. The Japanese or Chinese bow is subtly calibrated to reflect the relative status of the two parties. The way an English person does or does not shake hands, kiss or embrace someone, is traditionally very different from his or her continental neighbours.

Fashions come and go, of course. Erasmus in the early sixteenth century noted with approval the way in which the English kissed each other, unlike his Continental contemporaries. By the time I was a boy, kissing strangers at greeting or parting was taboo. Rapidly, in the last twenty years, continental kissing, usually on both cheeks, as well as hugging men has spread rapidly.

Of course, you have to be careful and with an unknown member of the opposite sex, or with children, it is probably best not to kiss or hug except in the presence of others who can act, if necessary, as witnesses. Never kiss on the lips, of course, except your partner.

Likewise, gestures have changed. The English, especially the middle class, were noted for not waving their arms to emphasize their speech. They were somewhat rigid and constrained, even their upper lips were stiff. They departed from this in periods of political or sporting excitement. Yet on the whole, the English can express themselves minimally and find waving of arms or jumping up and down bad manners unless in politics and sport. They also find standing too close is threatening. About a metre or two (three to five feet) is about right, which conforms very well with the distance customary in China, but is further apart than in many parts of Africa. You will have to study the variations and act accordingly.

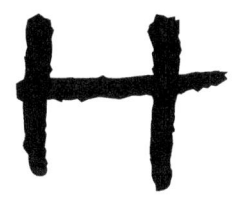

Happiness

'Man does not strive after happiness; only the Englishman does that.' So, wrote Friedrich Nietzche. Historically, the English were the only people who talked a great deal about, and pursued, that nebulous thing 'happiness'.

The goal of life in most societies was survival, or passing on one's wealth and position to one's descendants, or perhaps purity and salvation, or the exercise of power over others. The idea that the prime goal is individual happiness would have surprised and perhaps shocked many people as both extremely selfish and nebulous.

Yet for many centuries, as English literature, diaries and other sources show, the English have asked themselves if they are happy and, if not, have tried to alter their life to increase their chances of being so. They even turned it into one of their major contributions to political and ethical philosophy through the idea of 'Utilitarianism', that we should judge actions by whether they led to greater happiness or its opposite, against which Nietzche railed.

It is not easy to account for this peculiar pursuit of happiness on this island. It is clearly related to the early capitalist economy, for the pursuit of material well-being is both elusive and a driving force in the capitalist market. Consumerism and happiness are deeply connected. It is also clearly related to their individualism, for concern with one's own personal state of mind and body, which is not at the centre of the attention in most societies, is what happiness is mostly about. Almost everywhere, one is concerned with satisfying the needs and demands of others – children, parents, priests and lords – and not meditating on personal self-fulfilment and happiness.

Whatever the cause, it makes sense in England to hope that

someone is happy, and the search for happiness, as elusive as any other form of transitory emotion, is another English export.

History

The English have always been particularly interested in their past. Real-life historical programmes are among their favourites on television. The English have also produced some of the greatest historians of the last few hundred years.

Among the reasons for this is the unbroken continuity of English civilization over a period of about 1500 years. This makes the past seem relevant to the present, and indeed people still refer for precedents to Magna Carta in 1215 or the outcome of the English Civil War in the seventeenth century. The bounded island nature of England gives people a sense of a unified and uniform history which affects them all and consequently is of general interest.

Another reason is that English law and life in general is not based on timeless written codes, but on precedents accumulated through time. Customary behaviour today requires knowledge of what past customs were. What happened hundreds of years ago is essential knowledge for today. English history tells the English about who they are, what they should do, and was particularly important when they spread as an imperializing nation.

Furthermore, the English have the finest surviving set of historical records of any country in the world. These records spread back in detail and depth for over eight hundred years. They are there because they were never destroyed, as they were in other countries, in wars and changes of regime. The records were well preserved in the temperate climate and in the absence of white ants and other predators.

Above all, the magnificent archives are due to the system of devolved government whereby decisions were not just made by a central bureaucracy, but at the lower levels, including courts of law, parish government and local churches. This means that the history of almost every town and parish in the country can be documented in detail for hundreds of years. English local history is unparalleled in Europe or Asia, and the huge importance of the central law courts, which kept their voluminous records, has led to another extraordinary set of records of the English past. History matters and the English know and control their past, and hence their present and future.

Hobbies

'A hobby is an activity, interest, enthusiasm, or pastime that is undertaken for pleasure or relaxation, done during one's own time.' Thus starts the Wikipedia article on hobbies and I would hardly think them worth including in a book on the English, except for a surprise when a close Japanese friend once asked me about them. He asked why the English had hobbies and said that there was nothing equivalent in Japan.

I suddenly realised it is indeed a striking feature of the English, as George Orwell noted. Orwell wrote of 'another English characteristic which is so much a part of us that we barely notice it, and that is the addiction to hobbies and spare-time occupations, the privateness of English life. We are a nation of flower-lovers, but also a nation of stamp-collectors, pigeon-fanciers, amateur carpenters, coupon-snippers, darts-players, cross-word-puzzle fans.' Orwell also pointed out that private, informal, activities are central to the English. 'All the culture that is most truly native centres round things which even when they are communal are not official - the pub, the football match, the back garden, the fireside and the 'nice cup of tea''.[19]

Once I had been alerted to this, I began to notice that from early childhood, and much emphasized at my schools, I was encouraged to have as many hobbies as possible. These included collecting various things such as chocolate covers, stamps, coins and animal teeth. It included my most serious hobby or passion, fishing, that absorbed much of my leisure in my teens. It included playing instruments such as the guitar and mouth organ.

Later in life, when I was asked to give details of my work for inclusion in *Who's Who*, alongside the obvious questions there was one on my 'recreations', a posh word for hobbies. By that age all I could think of was walking and listening to music. Yet now I think about it, the question itself is odd cross-comparatively.

Hobbies are now widespread in the world, but earlier travels in Nepal, Japan and China makes me realize that hobbies were far less important among those I met and that schools did not foster and encourage them. Teachers did not realize how much hobbies expand the imagination, teach concentration and discrimination, and often give children something to be friends about, thus teaching social skills.

Why the English are such hobbyists is difficult to say. Yet the fact that for many centuries they have been relatively affluent, with a large amount of leisure, has helped. Furthermore, hobbies are a strong class marker and so played a part in the English hobby of social class discrimination. Hobbies being useless, yet absorbing, have also been a therapeutic antidote to the usual competitive 'games' and gruelling hard work which many lead through their lives in an individualistic and capitalist society. They are pools of rest and otherness, often 'a haven in a heartless world'. Now, of course, much of the hobbying is online.

Holidays[20]

In most civilizations, through most of time, the idea of holidays, usually accompanied with travel to distant places, is unknown or rare. This applies to very short holidays - 'Le Week-End' as the French put it, is unusual, though now widely spread, and the longer holiday of a week or month or more, is even more so. There may be religious pilgrimages, or trading expeditions with some sightseeing, yet very few peoples have had the leisure, wealth or interest in going somewhere far away from home to spend money, time and energy.

From very early on the English seem to have loved the idea of holidays. Chaucer's 'Canterbury Tales' of the fourteenth century give a graphic account of such enjoyment and English diaries, autobiographies and letters are filled with accounts of travels. They range from the 'Grand Tour' around the Continent for the rich, to the much more recent mass tourism of holidays in the winter to ski or escape from the English winter, to summer holidays all over the world.

These holidays are favourite topics of conversation. Even if you don't plan to have a serious holiday, it is a good idea to be mulling over possible destinations for your 'summer hols' to discuss with your friends. Where you go, how long you stay, how you travel, all are class indicators. Who you go with is likewise indicative. Usually the English travel with their young family or friends. They go equipped with sun oils and sunglasses and high expectations – not always fulfilled. Not to be aware of the high importance of holidays for the English is to miss an essential feature of their lives.

Honour and shame

Many societies show a very strong code of honour, revolving around men, and of shame, revolving around women. In the Mediterranean and South America where this is a central feature, it is called *machismo*, masculinity. Yet it is also widespread in Hindu, Islamic and in different ways, some Far Eastern cultures. Men should not overlook threats to their honour, insults and injuries should be avenged, leading to a world of duels, vendetta and vengeance. A chief threat to men's honour is the sexual vulnerability of their women, hence shame, and brothers and fathers are custodians of this.

What is noticeable about England is that it is as far from an honour and shame culture as it is possible to be – and has been so for centuries. There were periods of upper class duelling, especially in the eighteenth century, but the duel is unusual, as is the blood vendetta. A woman's honour is her own affair and she would not expect her brothers, or even her husband, to avenge threats to it with physical attacks on those who spread rumours or impugned it in other ways.

The recourse to threats to reputation, a highly important matter, but different from honour, is about character and trustworthiness, especially in the economy and law. It is fought through the courts in suits of libel and defamation. Any recourse to physical reprisals has long been forbidden in England. Everyone is, in the end, the guardian of their own reputation and must protect it as best they can. The 'feud' (a Scottish word imported across the border) is not a characteristic of England.

Horses[21]

Most people visiting England today will only notice horses at the edge of their experience. They may watch horse racing on television or at a race course. They may see polo matches or the frequent country events such as 'point to points'. They may see the ceremonial parades of horses on state occasions. Yet horses now seem rather peripheral, except at a purely leisure and symbolic level.

Yet for many centuries, the English were enormously influenced by horses. Indeed, horses have only really lost their major agricultural role since the Second World War. There was still a working blacksmith, shoeing horses, in the Cambridge village to which I moved in 1976.

The agricultural system could not have produced the surplus to make England rich, which led into the crucial agricultural revolution of the eighteenth century without the magnificent shire horses. Horses moved much faster than oxen and were more efficient, though they needed more food. Horses pulled the barges up the canals, the carriages over the terrible muddy roads, they drove mills, they provided the magnificent cavalry of the light and heavy brigade.

Horses, of course, were essential markers in the class system, for it was only the upper middle class and above who could keep them for hunting or jumping. They were used to quell riots and to impress foreign dignitaries. The Jockey Club at Newmarket was said by some, through the eighteenth and nineteenth centuries, to be the real centre of British power, rather than the House of Commons or the Crown.

Now, of course, many of the wonderful horses are owned by rich outsiders, but they are not begrudged this because it is recognized that they help to prop up the magnificent tradition of the land of the horse. Nor do the English forget that horses, as Jonathan Swift described in *Gulliver's Travels* (the Houyhnhnms - the sound of a neighing horse) are in many ways much more beautiful and better natured than humans.

Inconvenience

When George Orwell reflected on the differences between England and the rest of the world he wrote 'The beer is bitterer, the coins are heavier, the grass is greener, the advertisements are more blatant.' [22] This is probably still the case, but there are new differences springing up all the time and here are a few which have struck people from abroad to whom I have talked recently and usually somewhat shocked and irritated them.

What struck several were the old-fashioned machines for access to car parks and other amenities. From China, where very few people now carry cash but rather pay with an App on their mobile phones (or sometimes with a plastic card), to find machines exist which do not even take a credit card was a shock and considerable inconvenience. All visitors should beware; the coins are not only heavier but are still used.

A second Chinese friend was shocked and critical of the way in which most English sinks and baths have two taps, one for hot, one for cold, with the ensuing danger of boiling oneself and the inconvenience of trying to get the right mix. She was only used to a single outlet with two taps, making water temperature control much easier.

A third friend with a European background, was surprised that most English homes and offices, even the most recently built, only have a single pane of glass in their windows. All over the Continent, he said, double-glazing with its much greater efficiency, not only in keeping out cold and heat, but also noise, is standard.

All these are examples of the way in which a long history of doing things and making objects in a certain way, in a relatively slowly changing society which was the first industrial nation, has made adaptation difficult. 'If it ain't broke, why fix it?' is an English saying. The cost, both financial and in terms of a learning shift, is often too much and the English hold on to their inconvenient ways. They may even feel that a certain amount of inconvenience and effort are spiritually good for you, as suggested under 'Spartan', and they also like the old, and are a little suspicious of the new, as suggested under 'Antiquities'.

Individualism

The most essential things for an outsider to understand about the English is that they are individualistic. When we look at where all the rights and duties and meanings of English culture lie, it is in the individual. Consider the symbol of this, *Robinson Crusoe* in the novel by Daniel Defoe, stranded on his desert island, able to build up his world and be alone with his own creations and God. Robinson did not need others, even if he later welcomed Man Friday. Robinson was a complete economic, social, moral and political world in himself.

So, as English, we are taught through our socialization to be individuals. We decide what to believe, who to worship, how to behave. We are autonomous and full actors in every sphere of our lives. Our earnings are our private property and can be disposed of to whom we like, our rights to our bodies and other property are protected by law. We can decide who to marry, who to vote for, who so spend time with, who are our friends.

The only exception to all this is created by marriage (now extended to civil partnerships and long-term cohabitation without marriage). There we become 'one blood, one mind, one soul'. In such cases, the 'other' in this union now has rights in us, as we do in them. We are treated as an extended person, one of the reasons why husband and wife cannot testify against each other in criminal trials, though they can testify against their parents or children. Yet even within marriage, the English defend their individualism. Women have their property rights, and certain property tends to remain his or hers. Each has the rights to their personal space, privacy and secrecy.

It is not difficult to see why, while the family and other groupings are the irreducible atoms out of which most social systems emerge, this is not the case in England. For the separations and institutionalization of spheres has made it impossible in England to bring all the parts of life together into anything larger than the individual, or married couple. When conceiving of our world, it is oneself one starts with.

This, of course, leads into the 'lonely crowd' of separate individuals, very much like billiard balls bouncing off each other. If the English stopped here, it would be indeed a miserable, Hobbesian 'war of all against all'. Instead, the English have developed many subsidiary institutions which, while maintaining autonomy and independence, enable the individual to feel part of something larger, to act with others to achieve their ends and to control loneliness.

The most powerful is companionate marriage and love. Close to it, and often an alternative, is disinterested friendship. All societies have friendship, but with the fragmentation and mobility of England, friendship becomes particularly deep and important. In essence friendship consists of freely entered into, non-manipulative, relationships, the sharing of interests and emotions on the basis of equality. Friendships are different from useful contacts （*guanxi* in China), from the patron-client ties of Continental Europe or India, and they are for many English what gives life its meaning.

Inns, houses and churches[23]

If you visit the numerous small and larger towns of England you may be struck by the presence of larger buildings where you can eat, drink and have a bed for the night, collectively called Inns or Hotels. They often have a courtyard where, in the past, the coach and horses were kept for overnight travellers. There are thousands of these from the very small to the grand all over England and particularly along the main arterial roads.

There is nothing like this in any continental country. The reason is that for many centuries the English have been a trading and travelling people, with a large middle class, most graphically described by Charles Dickens. They are always on the move.

English roads were often in bad condition, but they were filled with travellers and they needed places to stay and eat and sleep, and the inn was the place. Even if they had family living in the town through which they were passing, they would probably prefer to stay in an Inn.

The inns are part of the wonderful survival of village and town houses in many parts of England. The old sheep towns and villages of East Anglia or the Cotswolds, or the seventeenth century villages in Yorkshire or Lancashire are among the special areas. Yet almost anywhere you will come across houses, and of course beautiful churches, which date back over three hundred years and many of them five hundred years.

Without wars, with widely distributed wealth, with good building materials of stone and wood, England has a better preserved medieval vernacular architecture than anywhere in the world. All this exists on a small island so that you can, with careful planning, enjoy a kind of time travel back through the generations of English life. You can do the same in the two old universities of Oxford and Cambridge, and parts of London, York or Bath.

Justice and fairness

In the majority of civilizations, might is right. In other words, the rich and powerful have controlled the legal and administrative system and the mass of the population have had little expectation that they would be protected by law. The rules were made by and for the rulers. Fairness between them and others, or locally between powerful families and individuals and their weaker, poorer, neighbours, was not to be expected.

One of the extraordinary features of England, related to the political and legal system, is that, on the whole, people expected and demanded justice. They trust, not entirely or always, but with some hope based on experience, that they will get justice. They believe that if they have been wronged, it will be righted. They believe the umpire or referee, if appealed to, will investigate and protect them.

'Fair play', that is abiding by the rules, both the letter and also by the spirit, has been highly regarded by the English. Much of their legal system was explicitly designed to protect the weaker, women, children, the old, the poor. It was concerned with 'equity', meaning fairness. Almost half the courts of England, until the two systems of Common Law and Equity were amalgamated recently, were equity courts.

So, on the whole, people expect that in all the 'games' they play, whether in economic, political, family or religious life, there will be underlying rules, underpinned by a firm and non-arbitrary system. Their Protestant God is also a guarantee that the just and the fair shall be saved, the unjust will be punished. Later we will see the implications of this for the level of trust in English society.

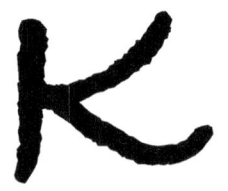

Kindness

Kindness in English has a derivation from the word for family or kin. It thus implies the way in which you should treat those for whom you feel empathy and sympathy. There is an implication of doing something without expecting an immediate or direct reward, or even being noticed in your acts. You do it to express a common humanity, to alleviate suffering, to encourage or support others.

Kindness is, of course, found universally, but what is rather unusual about the English is that the people to whom you are kind are not necessarily people who are close to you as family or neighbours. They may be people you have just casually met and will never meet again, or even people at the other end of the world who are suffering in some way. I remember a Japanese friend asking me why the English had so many philanthropic organizations for strangers – Amnesty International, the Samaritans, Oxfam and so on. He said they had not been known until recently in Japan.

There are multiple reasons for kindness being a highly praised virtue among the English. There is the Christian and especially Protestant exhortation to follow Jesus, to be like the Good Samaritan who helped an unknown fellow traveller. There is the highly mobile and individualistic society which is given strength through kindness and 'social love' as Adam Smith called it. The English have taken to heart the verse from the Bible in the book of Proverbs, 'Kindness is its own reward, but cruelty is a self-inflicted wound.'

William Wordsworth suggested that 'The best portion of a good man's life is his little, nameless, unremembered acts of kindness **and of love**.' The unremembered is particularly important, for kindness should become a habit, something one does not think about or mark and expect any return for. Kindness by instinct is the code of honour and something which it is well worth cultivating, not as a means to an end, but as an end in itself.

L

Language

Language both reflects and shapes a society. English language is now the international form of communication in the world and hence many millions are struggling to learn it, yet find it difficult to master. It is worth knowing about a few of its central features.

English is the original hybrid language. It is a West Germanic language (Anglo-Saxon) that has layer upon layer of borrowings and loans. It was brought by the people who settled these isles in the fifth and sixth centuries C.E. (once A.D.) but has been modified constantly by later waves of influence, particularly the Normans (French) in the eleventh century and later by the languages of its colonies and empire.

At first sight, English looks very simple and easy. Like the famous games of the English, the language has very few rules, very little obvious grammar, declensions, simple verbal conjugations. Yet it is the very absence of rules which makes it extremely difficult to master. Rather like the unwritten constitution of the UK, the language is full of unwritten rules and precedents that are not codified but are common knowledge to native speakers.

Its simplicity and flexibility makes it a perfect world language, but only by adapting the original language. Given the growth of English as a world language, we may in fact now speak of 'Englishes', in the plural. The US and the UK are famously said to be divided by a common language, and there are many thousands of variations or 'pidgin' versions spoken around the world.

The English language has both a vertical and horizontal dialect scale: vertical in terms of class and education and horizontal in terms of geography. Thus we cannot speak of a Yorkshire accent but rather an 'upper middle class north Yorkshire accent' in contrast to a 'working class south Yorkshire accent' and so on. Unlike most countries, people from different regions can basically understand each other, but they can also maintain a difference. Likewise the classes can speak to each other, but keep their distance.

Much like the people who speak it, English exhibits both a great rigidity and continuity in its use and form, its basic form or *langue* (language) but also huge innovation and dexterity in how it is spoken, *parole* (speech). The language tolerates the constant creation of new words: 'Brexit', 'tweet', 'hangry', and yet has foot soldiers who patrol good practice and write angry letters to the papers when they spot 'split infinitives' ('to quickly go' is an example of a split infinitive).

The language is subtle, rich and melodious and has been the tool for some of the greatest literature in the world, from Shakespeare and the King James Bible down to a flourishing world of children's stories and modern poetry. It is both a joy and a source of endless frustration to those who have to learn it, whether the natives or those from outside. As one of its greatest exponents, Charles Dickens, might have written, it is the best, but also the worst, the simplest, yet the most complex, the most durable, yet the most fluctuating of all languages.

Lavatories

All animals, including humans, have to evacuate the residues of what they eat and drink as urine and excrement. Yet how, where, when they do this and what they do with what is excreted varies hugely and is related to the rest of a particular culture.

In many Far Eastern societies, this evacuation was traditionally often a fairly public affair. For example, the Japanese up to the nineteenth century, built receptacles for urine and faeces along the sides of fields and houses for the general public to use, as the excreta were highly valuable for fertilizing the crops. I remember being rather shocked by the public *pissoir* for men in the middle of a busy street when I first went to France, where the legs and upper part of the body was visible to all passers-by. In remoter parts of China, you can still squat next to members of the opposite sex only separated by a very low wall.

The English have used their wealth and the presence of many domestic animals which provide manure, to develop a latrine system which is one of their greatest exports. The 'privy' or private room for evacuation, or the little shed at the end of a garden, were early developed. The urine and faeces were then usually thrown away, though sometimes used for vegetables.

The need to get rid of what was called 'waste' led to the use of water. The W.C. or water closet was invented by a former student of King's College, Cambridge, Sir John Harrington in the 1580s. The W.C. is now ubiquitous, reaching perfection, as so much else, in the high-tech toilets of Japan.

In terms of current practice, going to the toilet is still rather embarrassing in England, as well as in America where it is euphemistically called 'the rest room'. In England, the toilet is usually called 'the loo' nowadays by the middle class, 'the toilet' in the working class and 'lavatories' are the public toilets. The key is when visiting an English house or public place, don't be shy, just ask when you need to go.

Liberty

Liberty, or freedom as it is also called, is highly prized in England. No man should be a slave to others. All should be free within the limits set by the English philosopher John Stuart Mill, who wrote a famous treatise *On Liberty* and argued that we should be free to do anything that does not damage the freedom of others. Freedom of speech, thought and action, all are seen by the English as their natural rights. They know, of course, that absolute freedom is impossible, since it will destroy others' freedom, and that along with freedom comes responsibility.

Such freedom is often most noticed by people who come to England and become aware that they are no longer worrying about what government, priests, fellow citizens or family are thinking of them. Almost all peoples have lived in highly constrained and unfree situations. They live in one form of literal, or near slavery, where the pressures of the wider group oppress them, alongside an over-powerful government, clerics or the rich.

The English work on the principle that there should be a few negative rules. You should not be physically violent, should not deceive and lie, you should not treat others as people without rights. The rest is up to you. This is very different from the majority of civilizations which try to constrain thoughts and actions by generating countless positive rules. You must or should do this, that and the other thing. Negative rules of a minimal kind, as in games, give people far more responsibility and liberty.

London

All major countries have a capital city, which may, as in China, move periodically with political fortunes, but is the place where the central government resides. In this respect England is no different – the seat of government and law, and also of the economy (Stock Exchange, Bank of England, big insurance and other companies) is London.

What is unusual is both the relatively huge importance of London within the U.K., and yet it's curious unimportance. It is, and was, important because from the late middle ages onwards in terms of population and wealth London dominated the country. Often almost a quarter of the population were living in London and at times over a quarter of those in the country would spend a part of their lives there. London ways, ideas and wealth dominated this small island. You could say that England was London, London England. As Samuel Johnson put it, 'He who is tired of London is tired of Life'. It was the pivot for more than a century of the largest empire in the world and was relatively far more dominant than Rome, Paris or Berlin.

On the other hand, it was unimportant. The universities were elsewhere. The great bishoprics and cathedrals were mostly outside London. The judges travelled round 'on circuit' through all of England, so that much justice was local. For long the rich agriculture and much manufacture was away from London. The aristocracy and gentry lived most of their lives and had their power away from London. The great ports like Bristol, Liverpool or Glasgow were elsewhere. London was fine for 'the season' and for business. Yet the head, heart and spirit of the English was mostly outside London. It was the country, country towns, and country ports, that mattered.

London is well worth careful exploration since it is an amazing city, with pockets of the old alongside the new. Yet you will not understand the English if you stick to London.

M

Manners

A number of English institutions have the motto 'Manners maketh man'. This is curious, for it suggests that rather than wealth, intelligence, spiritual distinction or power, what is most important in constituting human beings among the English are 'manners'.

'Manners' refers to the ensemble of all aspects of interactive behaviour. They are about how you walk, talk, eat, greet, dress, deal with people in general. They are the full set of the presentation of the individual, encompassing etiquette, language and gestures. They even cover one's inner thoughts to some extent. The motto is often used in schools, for one of their major purposes, and that of universities and colleges, is to teach manners and how to behave. One essence of all manners is empathy, the ability to enter into the mind and eye of the other and to see yourself as they see you. Another essence is the English saying 'Do as you would be done by'. In other words, treat others as you would like to be treated if you were them.

In practicing good manners, it is always best to take your hints from watching local people to see how they behave. You will hopefully see, unless you are unlucky, that shouting and shoving, anger and abuse, neglect and intolerance are all 'bad manners'. Good manners take trouble, time and effort. They are not short cuts. You will find yourself, in a favourite saying derived from the Bible, 'casting your bread upon the waters', treating people with respect and behaving with courtesy, not just to get a direct reward, but because one day you may need to be helped by the manners of strangers. An obvious example is in driving, when you let another car cross, or a cyclist come by, you do this since you may one day be in their position.

It is impossible to list all the good and bad manners, changing all the time. Prince Puckler-Muskau's advice is as good as any, however. 'Of all offences against English manners which a man can commit, the three following are the greatest: to put his knife to his mouth instead of his fork; to take up sugar or asparagus with his fingers; or above all to spit anywhere in a room...' [24]

Masks

If you travel around the world you will find that many cultures use masks to disguise their faces. Sometimes, as in much of Southern and Eastern Europe or certain parts of India, Tibet, Africa and the Pacific, these are physical masks you put over your face, at a carnival or other special events such as a masked ball. Sometimes you just paint the face to eliminate all expression, for example in the face-painting of *geisha* in Japan or certain forms of opera in China.

It is one of the curious absences in England, except in a few local folk festivals or the occasional ball, that masks are not common. I have often wondered why masking (different from women's face covering) should have been uncommon. Among the possible reasons, I have speculated on two.

One use of masks is in intense, face-to-face, stable, communities – an Italian town, a small rural village of peasants and landlords. People know each other very well, but putting on masks in Carnival or other occasions allows them to distance themselves, to become anonymous. England has always been so mobile and filled with strangers that this need to turn very familiar people into strangers is less strong.

The other theory is that the English, as many observed, seem to be wearing a perpetual mask. We were taught at school not to show our emotions. Even when angry, hurt, or deeply upset we were to keep our upper lips stiff and our expressions impassive. The English have permanent masks to conceal their secretly ever-fluctuating emotions. The English do not need masks, for their faces are a permanent mask, and this is even more true of the Japanese.

Men

There is something odd about English men, not about what they are, but what they are not. This absence is not easy to grasp. If we look at almost all civilizations, there is a strong opposition of male and female. In the Chinese case, Yin means the female principle, associated with the moon, shade, hidden things, negative force. Yang means the positive or active principle, the sun, open, masculine. In this, men are innately superior.

In almost all religions, including the Catholic part of Christianity, women are inferior and men superior. In some cases, women have less or no souls and can only achieve salvation through men. In most civilizations, men have almost all the legal rights, women no independent rights.

In all these respects, English men have not conformed. There is no gender opposition built into the English language, unlike all Romance language where you have to know whether nouns are male or female. In England, women have always been equal in the sight of God and have an equal access to heaven. In law, though men are privileged traditionally within a marriage, a single or widowed woman is equal to a man. On the other hand in voting or pay, they have long been unequal.

English men have to persuade, not order, their wives or daughters. It is not a master-servant relationship. They have to share, not monopolize good things. They have to treat their women folk as their equals and partners. They have to show courtesy and kindness. Swaggering and *machismo* do not impress. It is very often clearly the woman who runs the man, rather than the other way around. It is important to realize this about the English and to realize that the true English gentleman is indeed supposed to be a gentle man.

Muddle

The legal and political system which underpinned the first industrial capitalist civilization in history, and the greatest Empire the world has ever known, was an unmitigated muddle. A muddle is like a tangle in a ball of string, a knotted, overlapping, confused heap of things or ideas. It would appear to be a disadvantage, but the English have not been dismayed by living in constant muddles, indeed they see it as an advantage.

'Muddling through' is a virtue and many of their favourite books and television series are based around people who 'muddle through', Captain Mannering in 'Dad's Army', or Basil Fawlty in 'Fawlty Towers' are good examples.

Whereas in many traditions virtue lies in clarity, consistency, logical integrity, making sure that borders are kept carefully demarcated, the English genius has always lain in the opposite. Their architecture is a jumble, their grammar a muddle, their politics as well as their law is full of fudges and muddles as can be observed daily by anyone who watches parliament or a legal trial.

As Alexander Pope wrote in the first version of his 'Essay on Man', life is 'a mighty maze without a plan'. The constant additions on top of past experiments, the strong and antagonistic individualism, the multiple sects and interests, the absence of a determining infrastructure, all are bound to lead to a muddled outcome. Muddled people with muddled minds, creating out of this muddle our modern, amazing, if muddled, world.

N

Night fears

Each civilization has its special demons or fears, things which lurk on the edge of the rational day of ordinary life. Although many English appear rather down-to-earth, practical, full of common sense and lacking superstition, they also have their night-fears.

One of these traditionally were witches. These were (usually) women, who were believed to have malevolent power within themselves with which through charms, spells and little personal demons, they could harm their enemies. Although the witchcraft period in England was mainly 1560-1660, and witchcraft prosecution was less extreme than that on the Continent or Scotland, witchcraft beliefs lingered on in the countryside in England into the nineteenth century.

This kind of witchcraft, where a person is in league with the Devil, and forms part of a secret organization which has cells (covens) and is trying to subvert the whole civilization through turning morality upside down with curious sexual perversions, flying through the air, blasphemy, is largely unknown in the Far East and was clearly related to Christian beliefs.

The other fear in England was in relation to ghosts, spirits of the unquiet dead, who came to haunt the living. The English were great ghost story writers and many an old house had its headless apparition or strange figure wrapped in sheets.

The English were also keen on astrology, table tapping and many forms of psychic phenomena and research. This reached a high point in the later nineteenth century, but many English still consult their zodiacs, read about their stars, avoid walking under ladders or feel worried if they break a mirror or spill the salt. All this is reflected strongly in their children's stories and counter-balances their normal pragmatism.

Oak trees

Each civilization tends to have an emblematic tree which is of both symbolic and practical utility. The Chinese have the most ancient and hardy of trees (actually a fern) the gingko, the Japanese the bending and multi-use bamboo (actually a grass), the Indians the peepul tree. The English national tree is the oak and its choice tells us something of England.

Symbolically the oak is very strong – the marching song of the British navy includes the following repeated refrain:

> 'Heart of Oak are our ships,
> Jolly Tars are our men,
> We always are ready: Steady, boys, Steady!
> We'll fight and we'll conquer again and again.'

An oak can last for many hundreds of years; some still growing in England date back to the Norman Conquest and before, one in Lincolnshire being over a thousand years old. Here they symbolize the continuity and durability of English civilization. Like the oak, England grows ever more complex and intertwined as it becomes venerable.

The oak is also central to English culture and survival. The great cathedrals could not have been built without the oak supporting their stone roofs. The ships which saved England from the Spanish Armada in 1588 or from Napoleon two centuries later, as well as building the British Empire, were made of oak.

The barrels in which the British distilled and stored their drink, in particular whisky, were of oak. The acorns were used to feed their pigs and much of the best English housing and furniture was made of oak. England is an oaken civilization, even though now oak is replaced with synthetic substances. The oak forests were carefully preserved and some still exist. They are well worth a visit, for example on some of the royal estates.

Patronage

In the majority of human societies, in order to prosper and feel secure, you need a patron or patrons, that is a person of superior position with whom you enter a personal relation. You give him or her deference, support, gifts and he or she protects and helps to promote you. Once you are powerful you need patrons above you, and 'clients' or deferential and loyal followers below you. Patron-client relations are widespread from China, through India to the Middle East, Mediterranean Europe and South America.

When Dr Samuel Johnson came to define 'patron' in his eighteenth-century dictionary, he described a patron as a rascal who claimed credit when no credit was due. Indeed, the word, except in the general sense of patron of the arts or literature, is little used in England. For it is a curious feature that although an English person often has a Master, which is important in all systems of learning a skill, as in universities with a 'Master of Arts' or doctoral supervisor, or piano teacher, or pottery master, patronage is something different. The long-term, unequal, constantly protecting patron, and the long-term subservient set of clients seems largely absent in England.

This means that while it is helpful to find people in positions of power and influence to attach yourself to as a mentor or if you want to learn certain skills, it is important to know that patronage of the normal kind is not to be expected in English society. You are protected by the law, you are admired for your own skills, though contacts of a fairly equal kind are, of course useful. You do not need to pay gifts or respect to a particular patron in England and to attempt to do so will cause suspicion.

Personal records

The English are arguably the greatest letter writers, diary keepers and autobiography writers in world history. The internal mental world of English (and Scottish and Welsh and Irish) men and women can be investigated through these sources in great detail for over half a millenium.

The diaries are amazing, not only the peaks such as the many volumes of Pepys's *Diary* of the seventeenth century, or the semi-diary of James Boswell's *Life of Johnson* and *Travels*, or Kilvert's *Diary* of the nineteenth century, but in a multitude of others, from humble workmen and ordinary soldiers up to aristocrats and rulers of empire. The self-examination encouraged by Puritanism, and the strong individualism and sense of self, are among the factors used to explain the thousands of diaries which still exist, many of them in print.

They are complemented by a huge array of autobiographies reflecting on a life. Yet perhaps the most wonderful of sources, are the millions of personal letters which have been written over the centuries and preserved in huge quantities, and many published. These take the reader into past minds in a dramatic and direct way, even more powerfully than diaries.

The reasons for this array of letters are many. The high mobility of the English, their early separation from their children, and in particular the far-flung empire held together by the imagined community preserved through letters have made this a supreme art form in Britain. I was forced to write letters from boarding school from the age of eight, and the weekly letters back and forth to my parents in India are an example of all this. Like my parents and generations of my ancestors, the letters were precious and so we kept them. One day, like the millions of other letters written by previous generations, they will go into an archive, alongside the many more letters I now write than at any time in the past, but now in the form of emails.

Pets

All societies keep animals, and usually classify them into three concentric rings round themselves – the wild, which can be hunted and killed, the domesticated, which can be used but are the property of an individual or group, and the inner, almost human group, pets. Yet keeping pets, dogs and cats in particular, has been observed by many outsiders as an English obsession. Like games, sports, language, law or democracy it has spread well beyond the Anglo-sphere world in recent decades. Yet for many centuries it was peculiarly English.

Many have speculated on the reasons for this. Was it because the English found themselves lonely when their children left home, or their companion in marriage died, and filled the void with pets? Was it that many, especially women, never married and the spinster and her cat became a widespread phenomenon? Was it because the English were relatively wealthy, with substantial houses and enough to feed their pets on?

For whatever reason, it is important to realize, as many noticed, that the English seem to love their domestic pets, from goldfish upwards, almost as much, and sometimes much more, than their close family. They spend more on their pets than on any humans except very close family, they started their Royal Society for the Prevention of Cruelty to Animals some years before the equivalent for children.

Please remember when encountering an English pet that you should treat it with the respect, and probably pretended affection, you would show for its owner's children. Pets are an intimate extension of many English people and so remember the old English saying 'Love me, love my dog'.

Philistine

Philistinism, named after a Biblical group, is applied in England to people who are un-cultured. They may be rich, even well-educated and knowledgeable, but their tastes in high culture are narrow and thin. They know little and care less about art, music, literature, but just get on with their job, at which they may be very good. The British Prime Minister, Margaret Thatcher, was often laughed at as someone who had no taste or discrimination, and the present President of the United States, Donald Trump, shows much evidence of being similar.

Friends from cultured Continental countries have commented to me that many of the English middle class seem disinterested in culture. They were more interested in making money, or playing games, or hunting or fishing, than in any of the higher arts. As a generalization, as dissected by George Bernard Shaw in *Three Plays for Puritans*, this is probably true.

Whether it is due to a residue of the puritan phase of English history, where waste, frivolity, display, worldly things were frowned on, it is difficult to say. Certainly, someone coming from a high part of another culture in China, India or France may be disappointed if they want to engage in conversation about the latest trends in classical music, modern art or the cinema. It is better to start with cricket or football and then move on from there. There is a great deal of wonderful music, painting, cinema in the U.K., but not everyone is interested in it.

Positivism and empiricism

It is not easy to grasp a certain tone of mind in each civilization, but we cannot understand the English without drawing attention to something which many foreign observers noticed about them. This is that they seem very rooted in this physical world in their thinking. This is what we mean by positivism, the idea that you start with the observable 'facts' of this material world, and then argue upwards (induce) from these. Another aspect of this is empiricism, that logic should begin with experiment on real phenomena, and then you can induce to general theories from these.

In terms of science, this is the approach advocated by the English philosopher and founder of experimental science, Francis Bacon. Start with the experiment and then move to general laws. It is also one key to David Hume's theory of the mind and senses, which starts with concrete sensations and empirical phenomena and works outwards from this to ideas.

All this is different from the history of French or Italian science, which starts, for example with Descartes, with certain logical premises and then deduces the material world from these in a more abstract, mathematical, way.

This mirrors many other aspects of difference. English law, for example, as we have seen, is very *ad hoc* and empirical, Roman Law starts with general principles. English business, English town planning, English literature, almost everything is pragmatic, fact-based, while in much of Europe or in Confucian China the systems are more systematic and consistent and are based on a set of logical premises which are worked out through the system. The English are different, as Orwell observed 'They have a horror of abstract thought, they feel no need for any philosophy and systematic "world-view".' [25]

Privacy

One of the shocks my wife and I felt when we went to live in a village in the Nepal Himalayas was the lack of privacy. Although as a child at boarding school I had lived a communal life, even then there were certain private things, and people respected your private space. In adulthood, my front door was a barrier and only with an invitation could people come through it.

In a Nepalese village, and over most of the world, concepts of privacy are very different to those in England. There may be very private areas, for example the seclusion of women in parts of the house, the kitchen in traditional Japanese houses, the forbidden city and Emperors' dwellings in China. Yet, on the whole, houses were permeable. You did not need to arrange to visit your neighbour or your wider family. It was quite acceptable for friends, neighbours and family to drop in and share the fire and perhaps a meal, and certainly a cup of tea.

The English in the past and still today are a rather private people. The fact that in my King's College teaching rooms I had eight doors between me and the people on the street is an extreme instance of this, but the desire for privacy is widespread. Even when I visit my daughter down the road, I announce my visit loudly and would not dream of wandering into neighbour's houses or gardens without their explicit permission.

Those coming to England are advised to find out the local rules of privacy, for even what look like open and public places, certain parks in London, certain Colleges in Oxford and Cambridge, certain beaches, golf-courses, rivers and moors are private. They are not always well labelled, since the natives assume that other English will know they are private, but you should be careful. Recently, the

English were both amused and scandalised, when a bus-load of Chinese tourists visiting a picturesque English village entered the cottage gardens and laid out their picnics on the lawns. Beware.

Queuing

One of the things that often surprised and either amused or irritated many visitors to England in the past, though the contrast is less marked recently, is the English habit of queuing. Many have noted that when a resource is in scarce supply, whether train tickets, shop goods, entry to a gallery, cinema or football ground, the English seem, without effort or thought, to form into a queue. They even queue pretty well when driving.

While many have noted the difference between this and the chaos one used to encounter at airports and train stations or busy roads in India and elsewhere, I have not come across many attempts to explain why the English queue like this and how it links to the rest of English society.

The explanation appears quite simple. Because the English are highly individualistic and subscribe to a belief that basically all are equal before God, the law and in the market, they need a way to organize access to special resources which is fair and neutral. You cannot use caste, masculinity, age, political or economic power to force yourself to the head of the queue, though you may be able to buy yourself into another queue as in Business Class at airports.

You have to take your turn, whether rich or poor, male or female, Earl or commoner. Time is precious in England, so that those who get there first have a right to have their early arrival recognized. It is extremely rude and offensive to 'queue-jump'. Only in emergency and with an explanation should you push to the front of a queue.

Revolution

A revolution, whether in politics, economy, society, or more usually in all of them together, is a moment when all the basic rules are changed. It contrasts with a rebellion or smaller upheaval. A revolution turns the game from cricket to football, from feudalism, to capitalism, from communism to democracy; a rebellion just changes the teams and perhaps the referee.

One of the peculiar features of the English is that their civilization has developed continuously through small, incremental, changes – through evolution, rather than through revolution. The only arguable revolution was the so-called 'English Revolution' of the time of Oliver Cromwell in the middle of the seventeenth century. Yet this was for many years known as the Great Rebellion and though, for a few years, it did away with the Crown and introduced some economic and religious changes, after 1660 and the Restoration of the Crown, the system went on as before, but with some modifications.

Compared to the great Revolutions which almost every other civilization has experienced, often more than once, most famously the French, Russian and Chinese (1949) Revolutions, the English 'Revolution' appears very minor. Likewise, the so-called American Revolution was a rebellion, which hardly changed the religious, economic or social system, though it did change the political structure at the top level.

So, the English have experienced no great divide or break in their history, except perhaps the Industrial Revolution of the later eighteenth and nineteenth centuries. The English like to improve, modify, re-invent and invent. Talk of Revolution brings to the English pictures of blood, chaos and ultimately an outcome which is worse than the present with all its woes. All this is particularly relevant as I write this in the 50th anniversary year of the '1968 Student Revolution'. I was at its British epicentre, the London School of Economics, at the time. Yet I hardly noticed it going on, and it is difficult to see that it changed much.

Restlessness

As Karl Werner noted, if we are looking for the quintessence of modern capitalism, we might choose one word '*Unruhn*, which means "in perpetual movement", but also anxiety, agitation - the English word 'unrest', but also 'restlessness'...' [26]

This fits the English case very well. Though the English can relax over a pint of beer, a fishing rod or a game of cricket, much of their life seems to be characterized by a constant desire to be doing things – making money, travelling, active sports and games. They seem a restless people when looked at from a continental perspective.

This may be related, as Weber suggested, to anxiety. The English seem, like other Protestants, to be filled with a sense of uncertainty about their salvation. They hope to be saved but they cannot be sure about this. Like other Protestants, they cannot buy their way to heaven through penances, masses and final absolution. They are not assured of heaven or *nirvana*, unlike faithful Muslims, Jews, Buddhists, Hindus, or even Catholics.

The fact that children are separated off from their parents and have to find their own way in life, as in Japan, seems to be another cause of this unrest and anxiety. You are never a permanent member of a group and have to earn and hold your place by constant effort. The English are the most leisurely, and also one of the most active and striving of societies. I was taught this from my first school with its motto 'By striving, to the sun' *(per ardua ad solem)*. Satisfaction and rest were like the rainbow's end, always just beyond reach. I was to be constantly vigilant, constantly on the move, hourly proving and improving myself.

Rites of passage

The *rites de passage,* as they are called in French, are basically those most significant moments in human life when a person is born (and christened or made a full human being), changes from child to adult (puberty rituals), is married, and dies and is buried. In most societies, some or all of these events are heavily emphasised and a great deal of ritual takes place around them. The family, in particular, marks the events with a great deal of celebrating or sorrow, and there are gatherings, feastings, giving of presents, chanting of priests, to take the spirit off to the afterlife.

Although there is some of this among the English, the major rites of passage tend to be muted. Some people explain this by the puritan, low-key, religion, others by the weakness of the family, others by the busy life which affords little time for rituals, others to the desire not to waste money. Whatever the reason, and with due exceptions, such as the marriage of a Prince or the death of an iconic public figure, a visitor should be aware that he will be unlikely to be invited to a christening, wedding or funeral unless he or she is a close friend of the family.

Anthropologists have noted that in many societies a marriage or a death affects many people, and the re-arranging of social relations which it necessitates needs to be orchestrated. In England you can marry in a registry office with just a couple of witnesses, or be buried in your back garden. It is a personal and private matter. Very few are affected except by personal grief if it is someone loved, or sadness if it is a more distant friends or colleague.

The basic social organization of the society is not much affected.

Royal Family

The British have one of the oldest and strongest monarchies in the world. The presence of a hereditary power structure, based on blood and some idea of innate superiority may seem surprising in a country which proclaims equality before the law and claims that anyone can do anything. Likewise, the House of Lords with all its ceremonial and hereditary aristocracy seems to go against the system.

It is indeed difficult to understand without a long course in English history. Perhaps one way to approach it is to realize that the English, like the Japanese for much of their history, saw the advantage of dividing power as much as possible. So, placing the ceremonial power in one part, the Crown and aristocracy, and the executive power in another, avoided the dangers we find, for example, in Presidential systems like the United States where power, which the English know corrupts as it increases, becomes very concentrated.

Or again, we can see that from very early on the English monarchy was odd. It was a constitutional monarchy, which means that there was no Divine Right of Kings, no absolute power given by God. The King or Queen has a contract with the people and is under the law, there on sufferance as long as they do a reasonable job.

The whole contractual system, enshrined in Magna Carta in 1215, displayed in the execution of Charles I and the deposing of James II, and formally described by John Locke in the late seventeenth century, means that the monarchy is accountable to the people. It is a system where the royal family amuses the English, binds them together, warms and sometimes endears itself. The English laugh at their royal family, but also feel themselves expanded by it.

S

Seas[27]

A visitor to England today will only see a few direct traces of the enormous influence of the surrounding oceans upon Britain. He will see the crowded seaside beaches in the summer, the yachting harbours, a few container ports, the fish in the meals. Yet this only gives a hint of the way the British have been a seafaring race.

The fact that Britain is surrounded by a very efficient way to travel to all corners of the globe, transport bulk goods with minimum effort, and guard against enemies, namely the sea, has been one of the largest influences on England. England looks remote on a map, at the tip of the Eurasian continent, but the seas meant it was in fact very close to all the world, from the Baltic through the Atlantic, down to the Mediterranean and across the oceans. Hence England is, like Holland or Portugal, open to the world. It benefits from ideas and goods from the whole globe.

The seas also protected England against famine since goods could easily be transferred to areas of scarcity and the fish and other sea resources were always at hand to supplement land foodstuffs. Along with tea and coal, the seas are in English blood and noone on these islands lives much more than about fifty miles away from the sea. This is something very different from the vast stretches of the land masses of most continental civilizations. The sea, liberty, creativity and equality seem to be associated through history.

Secrets and lies

Another paradox of the English is the way in which they combine a high regard for honesty, truth, trust and honourable behaviour, with a reputation for being secretive, dissembling, if not outright liars. The title above comes from a Mike Leigh film about the hypocrisies of English family life, full of deceptions, half-truths, attempts to avoid facing up to the truth. There are many other examples.

One kind of hypocrisy is the periodic public scandals where politicians are discovered to be leading double lives. The Liberal party leader Jeremy Thorpe's case of suspected attempted murder is currently in the news, and the Profumo sex scandal of the same time is another. Also, around then the Establishment was rocked by secret spying with Burgess, Philby, Maclean and others. Rumours abound and nowadays the focus is on sexual abuse.

All societies have their own variety of secrets and lies, but perhaps the English are notable for two reasons. One is that they set high standards, and have a puritan morality, so when the secrets and lies are exposed, there is more outrage than might be found elsewhere. The second is that in most face-to-face societies around the world it is difficult to keep secrets. Everyone knows all about you.

In England, highly mobile and an individualistic society has allowed people to conceal much of their life. Indeed, there is a widespread belief that a person has a right to privacy and secrecy and this is protected, though the English also have one of the most invasive popular press systems in the world. The law, for example, allows a person to remain silent, where in traditional continental law they would be tortured until they confessed.

A good deal of English life is lived with double standards, where people tell the truth, but not necessarily the whole truth. It is best not to probe too much, even if the person is very close to you.

Security

As an Englishman, I have been enormously fortunate not to have to worry about my security. There might be threats of nuclear war, or at a local level of strikes or unemployment, but for almost all the time I have woken each day to feel that I and my family and friends are safe. We will not suddenly find our business or house or other assets seized. We will not find that we are suddenly made penniless, with not even minimal social security help. If we are ill, we will be treated for free. Our children can be educated freely.

I was reminded of how rare this is recently when I talked to a visiting scholar from one of the richest and most powerful countries in the world. I asked him what struck him most about his life at home and how it differed from his months in England. He said that everyone in his homeland felt insecure. People looked to their history where revolutions and disastrous purges, famines and blood-baths were not too distant memories. They saw successful people suddenly stripped of their wealth or 'disappeared'. It was a constant ferment and nothing was predictable.

The difference lies deep in many aspects of English history and its fortunate position of being an island free from invasion and not facing periodic revolutions. Perhaps most of all, it is due to its legal system and the magnificent defence of the Common Law as protection against dictatorship, particularly that of Charles I in the seventeenth century. Although the language is archaic, the importance of the argument makes it worth quoting the eulogy by the greatest writer and judge in the Common Law tradition, Sir Edward Coke, who led the legal opposition to Charles. He wrote of knowledge of the common laws of England.

'If the beauty of other countries be faded and wasted with bloody wars, thank God for the admirable peace, wherein this realm hath long flourished under the due administration of these laws: if thou readest of the tyranny of other nations, wherein powerful will and pleasure stands for law and reason, and where, upon conceit of mislike, men are suddenly poisoned, or otherwise murdered, and never called to answer; praise God for the justice of thy gracious Sovereign, who (to the world's admiration) governeth her people by god's goodness, in peace and prosperity by these laws.'[28]

Service

Service means working for another person in a master-worker relationship of a personal kind. This is based on an implicit or explicit contract. One of the major forms of such activity gives rise to what are called 'servants'.

England was awash with servants until the early nineteenth century, in agriculture, in the home, in institutions such as schools. Servants were (normally) unrelated people, often young, who came into the home or institution and did many of the jobs which in other civilizations would have been undertaken by children or poorer relatives. For this they were given a contract, often for a year, and some payment, as well as food, lodging and clothing.

This widespread servant-based world dwindled from two hundred years ago, yet parts of it has persisted in various institutions, for example in the College staff in Oxbridge colleges or in boarding schools, hotels and in many offices. The vacuum-cleaner and washing machine and dish-washer killed off the need for servants in most middle-class households, yet even in my childhood many of my parents' richer friends had servants, and my wife was brought up as a child with a living-in servant in the household.

Although the many varieties of specialized household servant have declined in number rapidly since the Second World War, it would be difficult to appreciate the nature of the English without remembering how important they have been. From nannies for younger children and governesses for slightly older ones, through butlers and manservants, to porters and gardeners, English literature and life was full of servants. Many of the most insightful novels about the English, whether by the English such as P.G. Wodehouse's 'Jeeves' series, or by outsiders, such as Kazuo Ishiguro's *The Remains of the Day*, focus on the servant-master relationship.

The continuing presence of people who serve – waiters, porters, cleaners and many others, means that a society has to accept temporary inequality. Visitors to America found that the Americans were shocked by the implied inequality of servanthood. To be a servant was demeaning to a free individual, though slavery, of course, was accepted in much of the States until relatively recently.

The English dealt with the problem by treating their servants, on the whole, reasonably. Servants were weaker and poorer, dependent and not entirely at liberty, since they were under contract, but they were also protected since if you broke the contract with them by behaving badly they were free to leave, or even to sue you in court.

It was believed that it was important for a virtuous and honourable person to treat all those who serve them with kindness, respect, as humans and not as machines or animals. Nowadays, a smile or kind word or gesture and word of thanks is usually appreciated if you meet with the situation of servanthood, in a hotel, restaurant, school or even on a bus.

Sex

When he described *How to be a Brit,* George Mikes has only one line under the heading Sex. 'Other societies have sex, the English have hot water bottles.' The joke is caught in the title of a 1970s play in London, 'No Sex Please, We're British'. This alludes to the stereotype of the English as less fired-up by sex than their 'hot-blooded' continental neighbours, or, to the English, the lascivious people of other parts of the world.

There is a half-truth here. Scanning through English culture, the erotic motif is somewhat subdued. The carvings do not match Hindu erotic art, the paintings have less nudes than Italian art, the poetry and novels are mostly relatively chaste (though there are notable exceptions), the red-light districts and the pornographic industry are not at the extreme end. Their clothing is middling in its explicitness.

Some would put this down to puritanism, which placed a severe restraint on the fleshly sins and in particular illicit sex. Some would explain it by the public schools with their horror of masturbation. Others would suggest that there were plenty of alternative sources of pleasure, not just hot water bottles or companionate marriage, but arduous games which, we were told at my school, drove away sexual thoughts in the general excitement and exhaustion. We can note a relatively low-key, and sometimes repressive attitude, as explored by satirists such as George Bernard Shaw and Oscar Wilde.

Among the English, sexual innuendo, let alone sexist jokes, have to be carefully managed. Serious offence can be caused by sexual crudity of many kinds. The situation is now hugely complicated since while the taboos remain as strong as ever, what they are about is shifting daily. While old taboos, for example on homosexuality, have almost gone, there is much more concern with inappropriate behaviour with children, though this is very often about abuse of power and trust as much as sex. It is important to behave with modesty and care in this tricky arena.

Shooting and weapons

Many societies have historically been peaceful and weapon-free for periods. Yet even in the most peaceful for several centuries, Japan, there was a warrior group, the samurai, who routinely wore swords at their sides and practised martial arts. People in many other societies lived in a world of constant threat, whether from other humans or animals, and have weapons ready at hand.

One of the extraordinary things about the English for many centuries, clearly related to their island protection, powerful central government and law, and strong local government, was the general absence of weapons. The possession of weapons was strictly regulated from medieval times, which forbade the majority of the population from having any offensive weapons. Pictures, and inventories of people's possessions, show that these rules were largely observed.

There were tough punishments for those found with weapons such as swords, long knives and guns. The constables and the other law-enforcers until this day maintain a tradition of mostly being unarmed, except with a short stick or truncheon. Such was the absence of weapons that when the English Civil War started in the 1640s, it was found that there were hardly any weapons available to use in fighting.

All this is particularly surprising since this largely weapon-free English society (except for the rich who shot animals, or the yeomen training with their bows for foreign wars, and of course the battle ships bristling with weapons), has given rise to the most gun-infested culture on earth – the United States. There the early settler mentality, fighting Indians, wild animals and then the British, has been artificially preserved and now appears to the rest of the world as gun-crazy. Yet in England you do not need, and indeed should never, procure an offensive weapon, knife or gun, though of course when they went abroad in the imperial centuries the British were heavily armed and ready to fight.

Spartan

The word 'Spartan', derives from the hard-playing and hard-fighting part of the ancient Greek Kingdom on the island of Sparta, opposed to philosophical Athens. It is often an appropriate adjective for the English. Certainly, in the hard years after the Second World War and in tough boarding schools with mottoes such as 'A hard nurse of men', we were told that simple, rough, uncomfortable, living was good for us. Visitors to this day often find English homes rather bare, with hard chairs and beds, rough clothes and blankets, ever-open windows, simple and basic food.

Again, this has links with a puritan past and a streak of anti-sensualism. It is also to do with an aesthetic that stresses simplicity and minimalism. There is an abhorrence of waste, of conspicuous display and consumption, of 'showing off'. Here England overlaps with the Dutch and Scandinavia, other Protestant countries, which are also rich but keep their material culture well under control.

The newly rich from China and elsewhere may find English living is quite Spartan. The cars are small, the hotels sometimes a little shabby, the food and drink basic and the heating non-existent.

Forewarned is forearmed, as the English saying goes. If you face a particular difficulty arising from this Spartan tendency, try to explain the problem to your hosts. They will normally try to help. Do not suffer in silence. The locals will probably tolerate you as effete foreigners with different ways and give you an extra pillow or an extra fire and may even close the windows.

Summer[29]

The climate of England is temperate, without the icy winters and scorching summers of many continental countries like China or parts of Europe. The seasons blend into each other and the English cherish each of them, especially the changing ones of Spring and Autumn.

One season, summer, is the period of celebration and relaxation. Traditionally it was the time, after planting and before harvesting, when there was a little leisure in the countryside. It was the period when the professionals had their rest, Parliament closed down, as did the Universities, the Law Courts and the schools.

The richer went off to their salmon fishing and grouse moors, or to the gambling tables of the Riviera and their second homes, the poorer went off for their annual excursion to a seaside town. It was the time when many sporting and cultural events took place, which are still important for certain social classes today—Royal Ascot (horses), the Windsor Horse Show, the Chelsea Flower Show, Arts and Literature Fairs, Wimbledon (tennis) and the BBC promenade concerts.

For individuals, it is the time to visit country parks, have barbecues in the garden, relax and gather strength. Visitors will find May to September a particularly enjoyable time to be in England, even if the crowds and the not infrequent heavy rain and cold may sometimes mar the pleasure.

Sweet and bitter

Until I read David Allen's *British Tastes* (1968), based on consumer surveys and advertising, I had never realised that England can be read as a reflection of its older trading patterns and foreign influences. Allen points out, for example, that the west coast of England was ideal for ships from the sugar islands of the west Indies. All along that coast, you find the manufacture of sugar-based drinks and foods.

Bristol is famous for its sugary sherry drink – 'Bristol cream' is famous. Further north, Kendal developed the sugar-filled bar, Kendal Mint Cake, beloved of mountaineers. Further north still, Glasgow spread the love of sweet biscuits, especially shortbreads, which are still hugely appreciated.

Allen also pointed out that the middle of England, known as the 'Black country' from its role in the industrial revolution, was where bitter sauces were developed to enliven the foodstuffs of the new industrial workers, for example Worcester Sauce and Lea and Perrins Sauce.

To this we can add other examples. The East Coast of England is closest to the Netherlands, and there are many traces of Dutch architecture, drainage systems and even tiles, from East Anglia up to the East Coast of Scotland.

A similar effect of trade will, of course, be found in many civilizations. Yet because England is so small, yet with highly developed trading, the effect has been exaggerated. It is worth keeping an eye out for traces of the past tides of things and ideas which have helped shape this little country.

T

Taboo

There are two different meanings to the word 'taboo'. In general, taboo is used to mean anything that is forbidden. It is taboo to spit in the street, to harass other men or women, to let a dog excrete on a playing field, to utter racist or sexist remarks. There are endless small, prohibited, things though what they are in England differs, as we have seen, from other countries.

The other meaning of taboo, and the word itself (of Polynesian origin), came from the anthropological discovery that in certain societies things were 'tabu', meaning something much stronger than the forbidden things they had encountered in their homeland. The anthropologists brought back the word in order to show the unfamiliar bundle of meanings which it contains.

Taboo in this strong sense means that certain actions, and perhaps words and thoughts, if used or practised will automatically bring disaster. The tragic story of Oedipus, who unknowingly married his mother and killed his father, and was then hounded to death, is a famous example.

In societies with strong taboos, many apparently random things are surrounded by mystical danger. If you cut down a certain tree, touch a certain rock, eat a certain animal, then, even if you meant no harm, you would automatically be punished by some spiritual force which makes you ill, or kills your loved ones.

Perhaps as children, the English have such a belief, surrounding themselves with dangers and thresholds not to cross. Even as adults, they hold a belief of random danger; not spilling the salt, not cracking a mirror, not walking under ladders, touching wood when they make a predictive statement with some uncertainty in it. Yet, on the whole, the English are free of Taboo in the strong sense, even if their complex culture and social system fills their life with endless minor and shifting taboos which are constantly tripping them up, and even more so visitors to their country.

Taxation

Adam Smith singled out an efficient and fair taxation system as one of the three central causes which lay behind the growth of wealth in a country, and the history of England, upon which he based his theory, confirms his view. English taxation was, and is, peculiar in various ways.

Firstly, there is the extent of the taxation. For many centuries, the English paid far more tax per head of population to their government than any Continental nation or anywhere such as India or China. Yet instead of protesting and rebelling against this (except in the case of the American secession over 'taxes without representation'), paying these taxes was done fairly willingly. Indeed, the willingness, trust and confidence are shown to this day, when private individuals are allowed to assess their own taxes, to fill in their own (incredibly simple) tax forms with their income and expenditure. They are expected to, and, on the whole, do this honestly and on time. This is rather amazing, since tax evasion and avoidance is so widespread around the world, including by the very wealthy in England.

One of the reasons they do so is that on the whole it is felt that the tax is fair, that those who have the most, pay the most. Another is that people can see that most of the tax comes back to them and their fellow citizens in useful services – roads, hospitals, schools and defence. In most of the world through history, taxes were squeezed from protesting populations and very little of the money was returned, but rather used for the bloated life styles, stifling bureaucracies and huge armies of absolutist rulers and hereditary nobles.

If you live and work in the U.K., do not try to avoid or evade your tax duties. It is one of the obligations, even privileges, of living in a welfare state, and, as with many things, what you cast upon the waters will come back to you and others.

Tea and sugar

Some say that the English have tea flowing in their veins instead of blood. It is indeed true that tea has, and still does, play a huge role in English life. 'The good cup of tea' is an answer to most personal or national emergencies. Of course, this is also equally true for much larger China or Japan and now in many countries. Yet tea has a peculiar association with the English in various ways.

Firstly, in the way it is drunk. At first, tea from China when imported in the seventeenth century was drunk cold, from a barrel, like beer. Then, because the English had a large dairy (milk) industry, and an increasing import of sugar from the West Indies, and the tea that was imported from China was increasingly black tea, it was drunk hot, with milk and sugar. This led to a huge cultural change in English eating patterns – to the large English breakfast, the late English dinner in the evening with afternoon tea as a filler light meal.

In this process, tea elevated the status of women who became the tea masters. Women had often served ale or beer in small alehouses and pubs, but middle class women would not have been the centre of handing out beer in their own homes, as they became with the domestic tea ceremonies. The trade in tea furnished the major wealth of the East India Company and hence became the backbone of the British Empire, and it tragically led to the Opium wars and the destruction of China in the nineteenth century.

Tea also had a profound effect on English health, for tea contains powerful anti-bacterials which kill most water-borne diseases. Tea also concentrates and refreshes the mind and body and so was essential for the factory workers and miners who made the first industrial revolution in the world.

So, tea and sugar truly helped Britain with their breakthroughs to a new form of production (industrialism) and a new world Empire. It is a miracle plant in many ways and it is still an enigma why the British should have taken to it so strongly, and not the peoples of the European mainland.

Time

The English are the true Time Lords. This is not just because they invented the great Time Lord, Dr Who, but because they were at the forefront of the invention of modern time machines and still rule world time to this day.

The basis of the revolution in time was the mechanization of time measuring through the escapement mechanism, which replaced natural or organic time (sun, water, sand) by mechanical time. The device may have been invented in China, but one of the first, and certainly the most complex, mechanisms of this kind was invented by Richard of Wallingford at St Albans's in England in 1336. Subsequently the English took rapidly to time measuring devices, first clocks and then watches, and became supreme craftsmen in this field.

The English also developed the rule of time through the reach of their Empire which needed accurate, world-wide, standard time. So, they established Greenwich Mean Time, GMT, which is now the world-wide standard for all time calculations around the world.

Whether it was their capitalist obsession with saving, measuring and costing time that led to the above, or the above which influenced their obsession with time it is impossible to say. The effect however is not to be doubted. In England, time is money, punctuality is a great virtue. 'The Englishman is not covetous of money, but he is supremely covetous of time. It is wonderful how exactly the English keep to their appointments. They take out their watch, regulate it by that of their friend, and are punctual at the place and hour.' [30] People from other cultures who are used to the elastic time of much of the world should remember that it is very important 'to be on time' in all engagements.

They should also be aware that the widespread practice of emphasizing your superiority by making people await your attention, called *chakari*, for instance, in Nepal, is not an English speciality. People become very restless if kept waiting for no reason, so do not, as in many parts of the world, deliberately keep people hanging around for your attention just to emphasize your superiority.

Trust

Many foreigners coming to England have been struck by public signs of trust and honesty. In many cities, newspapers are put out in the street with a small 'honesty box' for people to put their payment in. People do put in the money, and seldom are the boxes stolen. Chinese friends were amazed to see the allotments in our village, with no fences and much-used paths beside them. They said that in China, the vegetables would quickly be taken. Likewise, people in the village put out fruit and vegetables, eggs and books for sale, with a small collecting tin. Again, this greatly surprised our friends.

It is all about trust, where trust means that individuals take the risk that people will fulfil their obligations, carry out their explicit or implicit promises, behave decently and honourably, even when there are no enforcing mechanisms at hand. It is a very variable quality and much of modern life depends upon it.

In many societies trust only extends as far as the edges of one's family, or to close neighbours, or members of the same caste. All these can be trusted to a degree because you know them very well and because if they break the trust, then other long-term pressures can be put on them through personal ties. Beyond these face-to-face, known, contacts, there is little or no trust. You cannot trust strangers, government officials, people from other villages or ethnic groups. You always have to be on your guard.

One of the extraordinary features of the English, as noted over the centuries, was the high level of trust and trustworthiness. It was not a matter of written contracts, but verbal consent and agreement, put in the English saying 'An Englishman's word is his bond' (a bond being a written contract). If you engaged in economic or other transactions you could, to a considerable extent, trust your partners in the same way as long-distance traders from Islamic or Jewish groups trusted their co-religionists. Here in England there was trust in non-kin, non-neighbours, even non-co-religionists. As Laing observed in the early nineteenth-century, 'In all the common business of trade, even to the greatest amount, mutual reliance, not mutual distrust, is the rule; and transactions in the ordinary affairs of life depend upon the good faith, the word, the custom of the parties, much more than upon legal deeds and written contracts of fulfilment.' [31]

Some were more trustworthy than others. Nonconformists, for example Quakers, were particularly trustworthy, for a part of their ethic (as was the case of most Protestants), was that God was watching you and if you behaved in a lying or deceitful manner, He would punish you. The whole of advanced capitalism and the highly mobile world of England depended on trust with virtual strangers.

This continues to a considerable degree and spreads to the non-English in the U.K. With occasional exceptions, and with a certain common sense, a visitor to England can trust strangers and one-off acquaintances in a way that was rather unusual until recently around the world.

Truth

One thing you could basically trust another English person with was truth. If you asked someone under oath in court, or in many normal transactions, to tell you the truth, you had a reasonable expectation that they would do so. This is again something which cannot be taken for granted and the difference was noted by the British when they travelled around the world. Although British merchants and missionaries noted how amazingly trustworthy and truthful were their Chinese partners in China, it was also a common experience to find that people told you not the factual, but the socially-acceptable, truth.

In other words, if we distinguish, as most languages do, between truth in the sense of physical reality, and the truth in terms of what the speaker thinks would best please the listener and best express their social relationship, then truth in most societies is mainly about social truth.

A well-known example is the puzzled English person asking whether a road will take him to a certain town. The Indian or Irishman says yes. Then the Englishman points to another road, and the native answers yes. In fact, all roads lead to Rome, as the saying goes, and both are true. Yet the English found, as reported in many colonial situations, that the answers they received were refracted through the power relationship, the family relationship and so on.

The idea that you could expect someone to tell 'the truth, the whole truth and nothing but the truth' as in a court of law, and do this even if it would damage a person's close family, amazed many of those ruled by the British. The very idea that there was a single thing called 'Truth' and that we will all see the same truth is laughable to many. This idea of the relativity of truth is not a product of the present, so-called 'Post-Truth', world.

In our post-modern and relativist world we are all more sceptical of the heavily positivist and empiricist view of the ultimate truth. We know that even at the deepest level of quantum physics, truth, like time and space, is relative. Yet the English are still shocked by Jesting Pilate's answer in the trial of Jesus, who answered 'What is Truth?', and did not wait for an answer.

Understatement and modesty

I have often been surprised when starting to talk to people in Cambridge about their lives by the degree to which they understate their achievements. You can ask someone if they play any games and they say that they sometimes kick a ball about or hit a ball with a bat. Then you later discover that they are international sportsmen. 'Are you good at maths?', 'reasonably good' is the reply and then you discover they are the Professor of Theoretical Mathematics and have won the Fields Medal, the equivalent of a Nobel Prize.

In fact, looking at my schooling, I see we were systematically discouraged from any boasting – it was called 'swanking' – from any puffing ourselves up. We were to be modest and measured. We should not overdo this modesty and become grovelling, but should understate rather than overstate. Then, if the questioner were really interested, they could elicit the further details of our true worth. It was all part of a general modesty and carefulness in all parts of our behaviour.

Again there are many reasons for this emphasis. Puritanism in general encourages humility, simplicity and an awareness of one's own lowly position. The English therefore do not feel that people's estimation of you will rise if you boast.

All this is very different from the situation in many countries, where you assert status and honour by puffing yourself up. The English admire humble 'Ratty' and not the boastful 'Toad' in *The Wind in the Willows* by Kenneth Graham. So, remember that humility, modesty, understatement, mixed with some self-irony, are much appreciated in England.

United Kingdom

One thing that surprises visitors to the United Kingdom is the fact that while they expected one, united, country, there appear to be four smaller countries, England, Scotland, Wales and Northern Ireland. They have different parliaments, different laws to a certain extent, different myths and very distinctive accents. How can they co-exist in this small space?

Recently, and in comparison to the serious confrontations when Continental nations are threatened with secessionist movements, outsiders were amazed that the English appeared prepared to let the Scots vote to leave the Union, something that could never happen with Catalonia in Spain, Corsica in France, let alone Nagaland or Manipur in India, or a province of China.

Basically, the Union, as in United Kingdom, is a voluntary, contractual one. It may have been brought into existence through force, military or financial, but it is now a club to which you belong, like the British Commonwealth. Like all clubs, there are rules and benefits, costs of membership and constraints on your behaviour. Like all clubs, members are there freely and if at any time they wish to leave the club, that is up to them. Perhaps it is a little like an English family also, where children, once adult, are free to leave whenever they like, taking all their assets with them.

What holds the United Kingdom together is some shared history, the Crown, the currency, defence, some laws and some joint political unity. They are parts of something which is not, however, an organic body. They are not like legs or arms or heads, without which the body cannot survive. They are like parts of a large garden, which can be separated off for other purposes. So, they are not joined together by the intense emotion found in many countries, where to lose Brittany, or Eastern Ukraine, or Taiwan, would be felt to be a violation of the whole national body.

Universities

Universities are to be found all over the world, yet there is something strange and difficult to understand about two of them, Oxford and Cambridge in England. I first realized this difficulty when one of the world's leading sociologists and experts on education, a French scholar, asked a friend to write an article explaining Cambridge colleges to him and his colleagues. He said that they were baffled by Cambridge and particularly the College system.

Colleges in Oxford and Cambridge are unique. Such organizations, where students live in an intense, bounded, community of scholars, where they eat, sleep, play, study and for much of history prayed, were once widespread in Europe. Oxford and Cambridge originally derive from the Paris model. Yet over time the collegiate system was destroyed everywhere, including in Scotland, to a large extent. Nor was it taken in more than a very watered-down form to the American universities founded by Cambridge scholars.

The double system of University and Colleges in Oxford and Cambridge allows people to have two allegiances and hence gives freedom and energy to the universities. It has produced the two most important universities in world history which still, despite having far less wealth than many of their rivals, are always near, or at, the top of world rankings. It is worth visiting one or both of them and reading something more of their history and culture in order to understand one essence of Englishness.

Urbanism

One of the more difficult things to understand about the English is their attitude to cities and the countryside. On the one hand, the English look and feel like city folk. Their way of life is filled with the tell-tale signs of 'urbanism as a way of life' as described in many classical sociological studies. For centuries, their diaries, letters, court cases and literature have shown concern with those quintessentially urban things; time as precious, fleeting and irreversible, not cyclical; space as neutral and not filled with carefully demarcated 'sacred' and dangerous areas; money as a universal measure of value and spreading everywhere; writing and education spread across the population; numerous daily contacts with unrelated strangers; constantly changing fashions in clothes, food, language and leisure.

With their bustling and highly mobile society, for a couple of centuries part of a vast world Empire, they were cosmopolitan, knowledgeable about the world, and urban values penetrated and shaped the remotest areas.

Yet with this they preserved the opposite, namely a resolute anti-urbanism shown in their preference for living in the countryside, whether in the dream of a small thatched cottage with climbing honeysuckle, or in small gentry houses with some hunting and fishing, or in the vast estates of their richest families, often built on slavery and colonialism.

Rus in urbe (the country in the town) is shown in the tree-lined streets and many parks and tiny gardens. *Urbs in rure* (the city in the country) is shown in their country churches filled with the tombs of successful business-men and imperialists. It is difficult to understand a totally different mix from anywhere else in the world, but it adds a certain excitement to the country, and a certain charm to their towns and cities. Their invention of the 'Garden City' idea, is just one expression of this.

Utopia[32]

People in all societies and civilizations dream about a world that exists elsewhere. Usually, however, this is in some after-world such as the Islamic or Catholic visions of Paradise. The English for some reason have not been much interested in Heaven. Most of us spend little time thinking of it, and when we do it is just a vague idea featuring clouds, harps, angels and a white-bearded figure.

Without Paradise, which comes after death, the English invented another form of dream or parallel reality, both existing, but nowhere in particular, namely 'Utopia'. The word which means literally 'Nowhere' or, as in one of its expressions in the novel by Samuel Butler, *Erehwon* ('Nowhere' spelt backwards).

This is in some way an adult version of similar Utopian stories for children, when the hero or heroine slips through a rabbit hole, platform nine and three quarters, wardrobe or other portal into a magic would which is often a critique of this world.

In the adult version of Thomas More's *Utopia*, Swift's *Gulliver's Travels*, or more recently Douglas Adams' *Hitchhiker's Guide to the Galaxy* or Terry Pratchett's *Discworld* series, the other world is not necessarily paradise. It has its flaws. Yet they do everything differently there. For example, in Butler's book, the inhabitants of that other land see the birth of a new child or sickness as shameful and to be lamented.

Death is to be rejoiced at, and crime is a sickness with which one sympathizes.

The English Utopia is active, sometimes optimistic, often full of fun, an attempt to improve this world by showing up our unfounded and unrecognized biases. The normal religious Paradise is a compensation and reward to make up for the unalterable sufferings of this world. Utopia is a call to action. As is its reverse, the dystopian novels, for example George Orwell's *1984*, or *Blade Runner*, or E.M. Forster's wonderful short story 'The Machine Stops', critique our world in a different, but similarly active way.

V

Violence

All societies have their particular forms of violence, especially if we broaden the meaning of the word to include not just physical violence to the body, but include symbolic violence, for instance in language, gestures, or even in buildings or ritual. In this wider sense, violence means any act or communication which uses force to attack and crush another.

The English have always paid most attention to physical violence and here again there is an enigma. On the one hand the law was very concerned to prevent any kinds of direct physical violence which involved individuals taking the law into their own hands. It still amazes people that someone who physically attacks a burglar in their own home is likely to be prosecuted. You should never be violent to another without due cause. So, on the whole, certain kinds of violence, vendetta, blood feud, interpersonal violent crime, are absent among the English.

On the other hand, the punishment for crimes was violent in the past, with public hangings, lashing and beating in many institutions from the army and navy to boarding schools. Public violence against animals was widespread as in widespread animal hunting, cock fighting and bear baiting, let alone eating huge quantities of them.

In terms of symbolic violence this is hardly consciously noticed by the English. Certain kinds of grand architecture, certain kinds of haughty speech, certain kinds of class behaviour crush those against whom it is directed. The whole British Empire, looked at in a certain light, was a largely successful effort to use symbolic violence in order to keep huge swathes of the world subjugated with minimal expense and physical pressure.

The English are in some ways the least – or perhaps the most – violent peoples in recent history and they have handed on their skills in this field to the Americans.

Weather

The way you greet and interact with strangers, or even friends on meeting them casually, varies hugely and the introductory conversational phrases used are indicative. I was much surprised to find when I worked in Nepal that the two greetings were 'Have you eaten rice?' or 'Where are you going?' Since I almost always knew the answer to both questions in a small village, what was the point of the question, to which the answers were always pretty limited? There is more sense in the Islamic greeting 'God be with you', but this does not elicit a reply, except the same greeting in return.

The most common English opening conversational gambit, often a comment rather than a question is, 'It's a lovely/horrid/cold/hot day, isn't it?' This has struck many outsiders as odd. Is it the constantly changeable nature of the weather which makes this such a riveting topic for the English, and has done so for so long, for in the middle of the eighteenth-century Dr. Johnson commented "When two Englishmen meet, their first talk is of the weather"? [33]

A part of the function, if not the explanation, for this greeting is that the weather is not personal, it is neutral. We all suffer the same weather. It is not particular to a political party, social class or family group. The weather belongs to us all. Commenting on it says nothing overtly about our allegiances or views. It is a way of rather non-committedly and casually affirming a common humanity. This is why it is essential that the reply be as much a mirror of the question as possible. If someone says 'Lovely?', and you reply, 'No, it's a foul day', this is rude and confrontational.

The very common greeting 'How do you do?', with many variants such as 'How are you', 'You alright mate', also has to be treated as a greeting and not a question. You can reply, 'I am fine', or 'I am alright'. But do not expect the person to be interested in learning about your real state of mind or body in any detailed way. If you launch into your latest disaster, it will cause embarrassment and perhaps astonishment, but you can reply 'How are you?' in reply, and again not expect an answer.

The way in which you make the greeting (accent, choice of words, stress in the sentence), and the way all these things are contained in the reply, as well as a few moments of further desultory conversation about the weather, will quickly establish much about the speaker. It will help you to deepen the conversation and perhaps the relationship, or retreat with honour if it is clear that the person is in some way not someone you want to know further. It will also tell you, if it is a friend or neighbour, whether they are alright, or need further attention. Weather-talk is an art. Like the English handshake, it both brings you close to someone, yet keeps you at a safe distance.

Women

My young Chinese friends, especially female, tell me that one of the things that most strikes them about the English is the freedom and confidence of the women. Even compared to the modern, well-educated and competitive women of their own lands, there still seems to be a difference.

This difference would have been much greater for long periods of the past. There was a European proverb, 'England is a paradise for women (and a 'Hell for Horses'), which bears this out. Economically, legally, religiously and in terms of education, when compared to their position in many civilizations (Catholic, Islamic, Confucian), English women appear to have been strong, respected and independent.

An English woman could own property (especially before she married and when widowed), sue her husband in court, leave money to whom she liked. She did not have bound feet, live in a harem or in purdah, cover her face and body over completely, or marry at puberty.

Of course, women's status fluctuated in the past. It seems to have been high in England in the medieval period. A reading of Chaucer's *Canterbury Tales* of the fourteenth century gives some idea of the feisty

English women. Their status continued high until the late eighteenth and early nineteenth century, when many women were politically powerful and well educated. There then seems to have been a dip for a couple of generations, and their position only began to improve again from the First World War and the universal right to vote.

The reason for their apparent remarkably high and independent status is linked to all the aspects already described. For example, English Common law did not, unlike Roman Law, or Chinese Confucian-based traditional law, recognize *patria potestas*, the power of the dominant male over his household, particularly women and children. Here the English were very different from the gender-bias of, say, the words and saying of the Prophet Mohammed, Confucius or numerous Popes.

Xanadu and gardens

It is difficult to fill in the letter 'X', but one of the few words that fit this is the title of Samuel Taylor Coleridge's famous dream poem, alluding to the fabled gardens of the Chinese Emperor.

> In Xanadu did Kubla Khan
> A stately pleasure-dome decree:
> Where Alph, the sacred river, ran
> Through caverns measureless to man
> Down to a sunless sea.
> So twice five miles of fertile ground
> With walls and towers were girdled round;
> And there were gardens bright with sinuous rills,
> Where blossomed many an incense-bearing tree;
> And here were forests ancient as the hills,
> Enfolding sunny spots of greenery.

This poem has always reminded me of the wonderful eighteenth and nineteenth century English country estates, parks and gardens, often modelled on Chinese influence.

The poem reminds us that gardening is a Chinese, as well as an English passion, from the grand scale of Blenheim or Stowe, or some Oxford and Cambridge Colleges, down to the little cottage garden in many villages. Or the 'allotments' for vegetables, which can be traced back to the Anglo-Saxons, and then became widespread from the nineteenth century onwards. The allotments have survived as a widespread hobby since then, even though vegetables are plentiful and cheap on the market.

The English find that gardens appeal to their practical energy, their desire to link to nature, their sense of something that refreshes all the senses, a wonderful release and expression of personal initiative. The English have been keen gardeners, sending out their plant hunters to scour the wonders of the world and then classifying and preserving many species of plant.

Yet their gardens are again odd, in line with the previous remarks on English aesthetics. The English have their stately, classically or Chinese-inspired, gardens. Yet they love to mix the symmetrical with the wild and tangled, their parks are half-tamed, half natural. They find the regimented style of many Continental gardens oppressive and dull, little to surprise or refresh. Only in a deep, perhaps untended wood, or part of a garden, will they find that 'green thought in a green shade' of their poet Marvell.

Y

Yes and no

One considerable problem in interpersonal contacts is how to say 'no' politely. Particularly if you are relatively weak, poor and vulnerable, and are asked to do something, or if you are asked to comment on something which you think a bad idea, or disagree with a statement, what do you say? Most people are faced with this often and it can lead to embarrassment, a forced lie, or perhaps anger in the person you are dealing with.

The Japanese in their highly integrated society, where huge trouble is taken not to give offence or be impolite, have developed a brilliant technique for dealing with this. This is to have only one word, *hai*, which means both yes and no. The interpretation of 'hai' is left up to the person who asked the question or made the statement. It neither endorses, agrees, submits, nor does it do the opposite.

The English, less extreme, method, essential for all outsiders to understand, is a variant of this, the device of 'Yes....but....'. At first when a proposition is made or question is asked, as in the way one receives the force of the other by moving backwards in a martial art, you say 'Yes'. Honour is satisfied. A few seconds later you then say 'But' and express your contrary opinion.

'Did you enjoy watching the royal wedding?' '*Yes*, the ceremony was extraordinary, *but* I thought it an enormous waste of money and there were many things I disliked about it.' There are endless phrasings and ways of putting this. You need both to use this technique, and also to interpret it when used against you. And you also need to learn the opposite, the 'No....but...' negotiating technique which is also very useful.

Young and old

Visitors from the Continent coming to England and America often noted how mature and grown-up English children seemed to be in comparison to children in their own countries. English children seemed to age must faster, be semi-adults from their early teens, capable of looking after themselves, entering into adult conversations, to a considerable extent independent of their parents.

This does indeed seem to be a characteristic of the English and the civilizations of the Anglo-sphere, and to set them apart. Parents and schools encourage self-confidence, independence and maturity. Traditionally in England, even young children could own private property, enter into contracts and even marry or go to university in their early teens. The young were sent off to boarding school where they had to learn to cope for themselves.

Paradoxically, the same observers noted with surprise that many older people were rather child-like. Older people would suddenly, at parties or festivities, or with their grandchildren, seem to become children again. They threw themselves with delight into childish games and competitions which would have severely undermined the gravitas of older people in many countries. Capek noted of the English 'They enjoy themselves like children, but with the most solemn, leathery expression; they have lots of ingrained etiquette, but at the same time they are as free-and-easy as young whelps.' [34] It is linked to the love of games; 'Sport allows children to become Men and Men to Remain Children longer.'

The explanation for the maturity of the young, and the child-like-ness of the old, lies in all the social patterns explained elsewhere. Its effect lie scattered through English society, from the ridiculous humour of the Goon Show or Monty Python variety, to the many wonderful children's stories, from *Alice in Wonderland* to *Harry Potter*, where an older person returns to their childhood world through imagination and encourages us to join them.

Z

Zen

Zen is a sect of Japanese Buddhism, derived from the main form of Chinese Buddhism (Chan). It is famous for techniques of mind and body concentration which eliminate all extraneous influence. Through long training, you attain to a moment of heightened being when all the world recedes and you are in a timeless moment of abstraction.

The English version of Zen is different. We can see that the English, as practical, money-seeking, capitalist, time-saving Protestants need something that takes them away from all these pressures. In other words, they need, and have developed, moments of calmness, concentration on the moment, escapes from the endless striving and competition.

One of them is the garden, and on a larger scale the national parks fostered by their unique National Trust. Another are the games and sports described above. The concentration on cricket, or catching fish, or in all areas of games and sport and hobbies, take the English out of themselves into an area of peace.

They find zen relaxation in the poetry they love, and in love itself which transcends and brings everything into a moment of clarity and meaning.

Some of their most characteristic religious groups know this - the silence of the Quakers, the inspiring English cathedrals, are examples of Zen. Thus, they are among the busiest and most harassed, yet also the most reflective, calm and fulfilled of peoples. Seldom are they more so than in 'Zen and the Art of Afternoon Tea'.

Some cultural rules by which I live

It is never easy to feel relaxed and at home in another culture where there are invisible rules which are never written down, but which the natives know through a life of training. This is a more pressing problem in some cultures than others. It is particularly the case in Japan, but also in England, an old culture with a set of unexplained and unwritten rules based on a strong class and regional system, often contradictory and often with no obvious justification. This makes it tricky to know how to behave. I had to learn all this when I came back to boarding schools in England from India, and have been learning ever since.

Basing myself on the preceding brief accounts of various English enigmas, and a life's experience of Englishness, let me very simply write down a few things I think I have learnt. This borders on etiquette and good manners, but is a little more than that. It is also obviously very personal. This is how I would <u>try</u> to behave, but others would see it differently. The rules and dividing lines are often fuzzy, and are constantly changing. The increasing ethnic mix in the U.K. and rapid technological and communication changes makes it even more difficult to be certain what the rules are.

If you are interested in testing these suggestions remember they are very personal, may not be appropriate in all situations, may be somewhat old-fashioned and middle class. Yet they may be an amusing list to discuss with friends, both from your own culture with those who have lived in England for a long while. They may endorse or reject them. The English are independent and individualistic and they seldom agree for long on anything. Do not be dismayed if they react negatively to some of the list. Choose your course of action for yourself.

Ultimately, this individualistic culture is a protection. If you step out of line, people may think of you as merely eccentric, usually a term of praise. Or they may be pleased that you confirm their idea that foreigners are less civilized than themselves.

If you do cause offence, an immediate apology will almost always be accepted, and the ensuing discussion of the reasons for the mistake may be enlightening. It is usually true that an Englishman (and woman's) bark is worse than his bite. An innocent misunderstanding or mistake is natural. Your cultural competence, like your linguistic skills, can quickly grow and soon you could be swimming comfortably in the warm pool of Englishness, while retaining your own identity safely. Good luck!

Here are some rules which I would try to follow myself when I live in the U.K., even if I too often fail to do so.

Conversational rules

I try not to talk about myself too much, unless specifically asked to do so.
I try to show as much interest as possible in the work and life of the person I am talking to.
I try to avoid arguments about contentious subjects such as politics, religion, sex, until I get to know a person reasonably well.
I try to use under-statement rather than over-statement. For example, if asked whether I write, I will say yes, I do, without going into masses of detail about my books.
I try to avoid using a direct negative when an assertion is made to me, employing the device of 'Yes.... But....' to indicate where I disagree.
If someone says 'Nice day' or 'How do you do' or any other conventional greeting, I answer in the same manner, 'Yes, it is a lovely day', 'How are you?'
I try not to praise myself or my possessions, letting them speak for themselves.

Behavioural rules

I assume that the person I meet is trustworthy until proven otherwise.
If I am shown a kindness (invited to dinner etc), I try to send a postcard (or email) soon after to thank my host.
If I feel that a gift is appropriate, I try to choose a light, symbolic, gift, which does not put pressure on the recipient to reciprocate. Preferably the gift should come <u>after</u> a person does one a favour, as thanks and not an implied bribe.
If I am puzzled or do not understand things or want to talk to

someone, I try not to hesitate to approach and talk to them. I have found that most people will assume that you know more than you do, but are very helpful when asked.

I enter carefully into friendships, stage by stage. I am constantly aware that the English have friends <u>about</u> things, shared interests and projects.

If I join a queue I would never try to jump ahead of others, unless there was a real emergency and I would then loudly explain why I am trying to get through to the front.

I would never touch another person's child without the consent of their parent or guardian except in an emergency.

I try to pay my taxes and all state and local charges fully and promptly.

I trust the police and would report crimes to them, even if they were committed by people I know and like, if the crimes are serious.

I do not barter for goods, trying to get the seller to lower the price. The only situation where I might contemplate this is in an open-air market or second-hand shop.

I try not to throw any piece of non-degradable litter anywhere, whether in the street or out of a car, and in my own village would try to pick up and dispose of litter.

If I am having dinner, I try not to take or accept too large a helping of food or wine, as I do not want to waste anything. I would not hesitate to ask for more if I am still hungry, though I would not help myself. Asking for more is a compliment.

If I am offered food or drink I do not want, I politely explain that I do not eat or drink this, for religious, social or other reasons. With an explanation people are not offended.

If I am eating with people who are using an unfamiliar set of utensils, glasses etc, I watch carefully how they use these and follow a few seconds after they have shown me how.

I try not to be late for appointments with people. Five minutes is acceptable on the whole, ten minutes starts to be a problem and longer than that needs a good reason.

I try to treat all those I meet with courtesy and respect. This applies to those much younger, or the very elderly, people of the opposite sex, people who appear poor, those from all ethnic groups, and all those who serve me (porters, servants, waiters, drivers).

I try to avoid ordering people to do things, but rather to ask them to do so. This involves starting with a 'please' and ending with a 'thank you'. This applies to all, including friends and all members of one's family.

I am aware that many places are private, even if there are no signs saying 'private property', so I try to ascertain before I enter them whether I may do so.

I have never carried a weapon in my life, except when I was doing military training, or playing as a child.

I try to tell the truth when asked a question or making an observation. If the truth will cause real trouble and pain, then I try not to tell a direct lie, but am sometimes 'economical' with the truth - telling part, but not all of, the truth.

I never use physical force if I can avoid it, against humans or other animals. I used to fish, but find even that not very enjoyable.

Some further reading on the English A-Z

A few books that have helped me to understand the English

Ernest Barker (ed.), *The Character of England* (1947)
Luigi Barzini, *The Europeans* (1983)
James, C. Bennett, *The Anglosphere Challenge* (2004)
D.W. Brogan, *The English People, Impressions & Observations* (1944)
Bill Bryson, *Notes from a small island* (1993)
Karel Capek, *Letters from England* (1925; 2001)
Ralph Waldo Emerson, *English Traits* (Boston, 1884)
Kate Fox, *Watching the English; The Hidden Rules of English Behaviour* (2005)
François Guizot, *The History of Civilization in Europe* (1846; Penguin edn., 1997)
J.H. Huizinga, *Confessions of a European in England* (1958)
Paul Langford, *Englishness Identified* (Oxford, 2000)
A.G. Macdonell, *England their England* (1933; 2012)
George Mikes, *How to be a Brit* (1984)
Hugh Miller, *First Impressions of England and its People* (3rd edn., 1853)
Erin Moore, *That's Not English* (2015)
George Orwell, *The Lion and the Unicorn* (1941; 1982)
Jeremy Paxman, *The English* (Penguin, 1999)
Nikolaus Pevsner, *The Englishness of English Art* (1956)
François de la Rochefoucauld, *A Frenchman in England, 1784* (1933), trans and introduced by Jean Marchand and S.C. Roberts
W. B. Rye (ed.), *England as seen by Foreigners; in the days of Elizabeth and James the First* (1865; 1967)
César de Saussure, *A Foreign View of England in the Reigns of George I and George II* (1902), trans Madame van Muyden
Hippolyte Taine, *Notes on England* (1957), trans. Edward Hyams
Keith Thomas, *Man and the Natural World* (1983)
Alexis de Tocqueville, *Journeys to England and Ireland* (New York, 1968), ed. J.P.Mayer, tr. George Lawrence and K.P.Mayer
Claudio Veliz, *The New World of the Gothic Fox* (California, 1994)
Francesca M. Wilson (ed.), *Strange Island; Britain through Foreign Eyes* 1395-1940 (1955)

My books on the English

Witchcraft in Tudor and Stuart England; a regional and comparative study (1970)
The Family Life of Ralph Josselin; an essay in historical anthropology (1970)
The Origins of English Individualism; the family, property and social transition (1978)
The Justice and the Mare's Ale; law and disorder in seventeenth century England (1981)
A Guide to English Historical Records (1983)
Marriage and Love in England 1300-1840 (1986)
The Culture of Capitalism (1987)
The Savage Wars of Peace; England, Japan and the Malthusian Trap (1997)
Letters to Lily; on how the world works (2005)
The Invention of the Modern World (2014)
China, Japan, Europe and the Anglo-sphere; A comparative analysis (2018)
Reflections on Cambridge (2018)
The Peculiarity of the English (forthcoming)

Acknowledgements

I am grateful to all those who have read and commented on parts of this little book, including James O'Sullivan and, especially, Sarah Harrison, with whom I have discussed many of these topics over the years and shared many adventures in pursuit of wider views on the English.

I have learnt a great deal about what it is to be English from working and travelling across China with young Chinese friends and I especially thank Wang Zilan, Xu Bei, Ma Xiao, Qin Yuchen and Li Shuo for their constant friendship and advice. Minister Counsellor Xiang Xiaowei was kind enough to read parts of this text and suggested several topics, based on his experience in the U.K., which I have included.

Especial thanks to Fabienne Bonnet, Bye-Fellow of Homerton College, for checking the text and for a number of helpful comments from a French angle which I have incorporated mainly in the footnotes (FB).

Professor Mark Turin read the text carefully, suggested a number of valuable deletions and additions, and provided most of the ideas for the section on language. I am particularly grateful to him for his supportive comments.

NOTES

[1] Claudio Veliz, *The New World of the Gothic Fox* (1994), 116

[2] Alexis de Tocqueville, *Journeys to England and Ireland,* (1968), ed. J. P. Mayer, xviii

[3] Ralph Waldo Emerson, *English Traits* (1884), 42, 75; George Orwell, *The Lion and the Unicorn* (1941), 46

[4] David Hume, *Essays, Literary, Moral and Political,* (c.1870), 122

[5] François de la Rochefoucauld, *A Frenchman in England,* (1784), trans and introduced by Jean Marchand and S.C. Roberts (1933), 92

[6] Cammaerts in Francesca M. Wilson (ed.), *Strange Island: Britain through Foreign Eyes 1359-1940* (1955), 251

[7] The French nation's favourite television series about the English is *Chapeau Melon et Bottes de Cuir*. An offshoot of the James Bond films. (FB)

[8] Count Pecchio in Wilson, *Strange Island*, 178

[9] In France there are cliques, but they are based on family clans rather than associations. (FB)

[10] France's collective memory remains fixed on mines as crucibles of strife and poverty, with the celebrated novel by Emile Zola, *Germinal*. (FB)

[11] Whereas in France 'flashers' are as common as flies and wasps, I have only come across one in forty-five years of living in England. This was on the way to Grantchester. Later on that day the man was arrested, and the incident reported in the local paper. More interestingly, I once crossed paths with a completely naked man on his bicycle: a streaker. This was not 'flashing'. It was a daring act of freedom. (FB)

[12] In England water and wine glasses always sit on the right-hand side of your plate, because of the bread-plate, taking pride of place, on the other side even though you might be given only one bread roll through the entire meal. Although traditionally there is no bread plate in France-- people place their slices of bread on the tablecloth – the higher the social scales, the closer our two cultures become. Nevertheless, it is true that the French are traditionally hermetic to foreign cuisine. (FB)

[13] George Orwell, *The Lion and the Unicorn* (1941), 119

[14] Hippolyte Taine, *Notes on England* (1957 edn.), 290

[15] The words 'sorry', 'please' and 'thank you' are commonly used in English, as ways of showing attentiveness to others, and they leave you a space, not to be underestimated.

[16] Karl Marx, *Grundrisse*, trans. Martin Nicolaus (1973), 163

[17] Emerson, *English Traits*, 116

[18] The French have a completely different understanding of 'Le Vert anglais'. A Morgan sports car, a Triumph Bonneville motorcycle, or household paint for front doors and gates. Le vert anglais implies style, something chic, elegant. (FB)

[19] Orwell, *Lion and Unicorn*, 39

[20] Most of the French holidays follow the liturgical year, except of course 14th July, and May Day, La Fête du travail' when no one is working. There is no term for 'a bank holiday'. (FB)

[21] In the late eighteen seventies France, women, not horses, used to pull barges up canals. (FB)

[22] Orwell, *Lion and Unicorn*, 36

[23] How different houses can look to a visitor from outside Britain. From rows (and rows) of terraced-houses in suburbs, to the pretty cottages resembling those in French coastal villages; to the highly symbolic use of rooms in England. To be invited to sit in the front-room in a miners' house would have been a mark of respect. This was also the room where a coffin would be laid. (FB)

[24] In Wilson, *Strange Island*, 175

[25] Orwell, *Lion and Unicorn*, 38

[26] In John Hall and Michael Mann (eds.), *Europe and the Rise of Capitalism (1988)*, 173

[27] One of my favourite entries, as a citizen from inland France. Finding flocks of seagulls on Parker's Piece, Cambridge in winter is extraordinary. They are the equivalent of our frogs and pine cones which can predict the weather. It also means that the sea in England is never very far away, a huge difference with China and Europe. (FB)

[28] Edward Coke, *Reports* (c.1777), vol. II, preface

[29] Although the climate may be known in England as 'temperate', the distinction between winter and spring is very strongly marked by the English. From young people going out in T-shirts (when most of us are still wearing hats and coats), to their delightful basking on Parker's Piece, Cambridge. This distinct note of spring when it comes is mentioned everywhere by everyone. It seems a hallmark of living in

England. (FB)

[30] Count Pecchio in Wilson, *Strange Island*, 178

[31] Samuel Laing, *Observations on the Social and Political State of the European People in 1848 and 1849* (1850), 290

[32] Under this heading one can be reminded of the Guild of St George, an English utopian society based on Ruskin's ideas of rural economy and the struggle against industrialism. (FB)

[33] Samuel Johnson in *The Penguin Dictionary of Quotations* (1960), eds. J.M. and M.J. Cohen, 213

[34] Capek in Wilson, *Strange Island*, 247

Printed in Great Britain
by Amazon